THE PERFECT MAN

THE PERFECT MAN

LOUIS MCCRAY

Louis Mccray

The Perfect Man

All rights reserved
Copyright © 2024 by **Louis Mccray**

Published by Spines
ISBN: 979-8-89569-023-9

A man, an individual human, a bipedal primate mammal that is anatomically related to the great apes but distinguished especially by notable development of the brain with a resultant capacity for articulate speech and abstract reasoning and is the sole living representative of the hominid family.

Perfect, having all the required or desirable elements, qualities or characteristics; as good as it is possible to be. Absolute; complete, make something completely free from faults or defects, or as close to such conditions as possible.

Is there such a thing as a perfect man?

This is the big question. A man to me is not a superhero that saves the day from crime and keeps the world safe from disasters or a person who turns every woman's eye because they think he's the closest replica to a God, mind, soul and body. A man to me is a real human being that does his best to conquer or control any situation thrown at him no matter how difficult he's going to try to be as successful as he can to accomplish this task, Get the job done no matter the cost.

The type of person that demands respect because he's strong minded, triple plus if his body and looks match his character such as a perfect man.

Unfortunately all men are not born with that dominant DNA that a woman drools over. We all come in different shapes and sizes. Some light bulbs shine bright and some are duller than the Sun hitting the ground like the horizons making it dark and gloomy as the day turns to night. Should they be condemned because they are not perfect, shouldn't they have the right to love and good fortune, kids, a pet or two, a house with a white picket fence. Sad to say life is just not like that. The men that I know kinda have to forge their paths, some didn't have the opportunities that others had such as finishing school and getting a six figure job out the gate.

Nuh, they had kids too early, messed up parents if they had parents at all. Half their family was addicts and the other half was barely present in their lives so they veered to that street life, whatever that meant to them to make ends meet to take care of their life situations. Everyone always says you have a choice in life but sometimes your neighborhood ain't so neighborly and you have to be a man earlier than expected and adjust to your environment or all is lost.

A few facts about the hood and there all over the world, not just in the Bronx, New York where I reside. You have a 40 to 50 percent chance of making it out or becoming a success. Success is like an image you see in a magazine or on television.. A prayer and a dream that will never come true if you don't play the game right. You're truly blessed if you have a powerful, knowledgeable person in your ear guiding you through this obstacle course of life. I personally thank God everyday i wake up as the man that i am for another shot, another chance to chase my dreams for me and my family no matter how old I get or how hard I struggle I wake up, sit up, grab these legs stand up get on my knees and thank the almighty for another shot at redemption because I've been thru some things like everybody else i'm not no better than anybody else and i just want to win just like everybody else. I could've been a rapper too, I went left, Sorry!

But, back to a perfect man, is there really such a person? I believe in change, you can definitely change your circumstances whatever they may be, learn from them and make yourself better. Is love perfect, life sure is not, what about death, is there a perfect way to die? We.re not born perfect so how can we claim to be perfect? What is perfect to you, I know what a woman thinks a perfect man should be, smart, intelligent, there is a difference trust me. Handsome, well-endowed; rich don't have to be wealthy, there is a difference but good enough to serve her dreams of being attended to on a silver platter you get the picture.

A man is the breadwinner and the woman stays home and takes care of the kids and the family. Maybe in the early 1900's. In 1935, President Franklin D. Roosevelt proposed to Congress economic security legislation embodying the recommendations of a specially created Committee of Economic Security. There followed the passage of the Social Security Act, signed into law August 14,1935. These acts were the beginning of what we now know as Welfare.

That was for the white economy of course, by the time black people got to figure it out i believe this was the beginning of broken homes. Once women figured out they don't need their abusive, lying, cheating husbands to take care of their households any more. I'm going to apply for welfare which forces the men out because u cant have steady income coming into any household to get it. You have to be broke with kids, the more kids the marreir and if your man works and lives at the residence, Bye Niga i need my stamps.

O yall didnt know welfare broke up happy homes, that was the beginning of, Im a single mother to this day. I didn't have a father he left when I was two, I grew up on welfare, yeah! The government opened that door my guy, facts. Did this make a man stronger or weaker? It depends on the situation. A Lot of great men fought in the army and died. The others came home and got hooked on drugs like Cocaine and Heroin. Then they put a liquor store on every block and sold trucks filled with guns to the drug dealers, pimps and robbers. Built projects to stack us up like sardines, put schools in the middle of that and told corrupt cops to get orders so they can fill up the new jails they created. Its elimination of a race at its finest, not just the blacks either you had the Hispanics couple of Mexicans and Asians too. The Chinese people always had their restaurants but their kids looked hurt too, I'm just saying. The American government wasn't built for the minorities at all. Why do you think it was so hard to move out the hood into a Caucasian Suburban neighborhood even if you clearly had the money it wasn't happening fam!

Personally, I was raised the same way, welfare, poor, father went to jail for life when I was eleven, moms was a crack addict. I had to scrape the pavement to get my paper, I packed bags, cleaned out stores, helped drug dealers bottle up, stole, robbed, cut school to put supermarket brochures in the projects door to door. Anything that can give me a buck to buy the things I wanted without begging. I would never do that. I still had my pride but I was only a kid for ten years of my life. After that I had to step up and feed my sisters and help my moms anyway I could. I did have some great women in my life that taught me love and respect for not just women but people altogether. My Grandmother Katherine from my fathers side taught me church and the bible and who God was to our family. My aunts, his sisters, twin Louise and youngest sister Yvonne. Louise taught me my book smarts. She always made sure I understood that my education was most important for the future of not just me but for the McCray family in general. While Auntie Yvonne taught me the street side how to be down to earth and don't let nobody play you, how not to be no sucker in these streets because the streets could suck the life out of you on God! One thing that's the most important is that I can't even deny that everyone taught me Love. Both sides of the family gave me love and respect so that just carried on to my adulthood.

People love the love I give some say it's too much. I need to learn to hate a little more but that's not in me. I will always spread love and be the best person I can be to others if I know you well or not. Don't get it twisted though i'm not a sucker but people I love do find it easy to take my kindness and use it to their advantage on me i'll admit that but I'm still a Capricorn so if you cross me too much I'm done. Ain't no sorry or being friends later you'll never get that close to me again eternally not physically i may have to work with you but dont fuck with you and you will know it.

I'm far from the perfect man but I can write a book to teach a young man or any man for that matter to read, learn and find out how to understand today's woman so he won't waste his time or her time having these stress filled relationships filled with kids that get hurt by them. You have family members that can get hurt even killed because you're putting them in danger, there kids in danger buy forcing these toxic entanglements for a heated night of passion you can go to jail, lose thousands of dollars, stop careers, have to move or maybe the ultament sacrifice your own life on the line just because evolution proves we have to evolve and create to live on. Everyone feels they need someone to be complete, someone to love and grow old with and you can. Everyone deserves love but what do you do if you made a bad choice, kids are in the picture now, your mother in law hates your guts, your father in law wants to shoot you because his daughter is crying everyday.

Life isn't all it's cracked up to be but from all my horrible experiences i've had time to think about all my mistakes without following my fathers path and doing a long prison bid. I've come to the conclusion that you have to slow down and learn yourself first. Learn your likes and dislikes before you commit to anything long term. For my older comrades all you need to do is find God and make peace with everyone you love in your life but for my young brothers if you want to be close to a perfect man all you have to do is learn about yourself. The type of person you are, your weaknesses, your strengths, what you like about women, if you even like women or not. That's a big topic in today's world. If you're having sex, protect yourself so you have less mistakes in the future and wont have children before you finish your schooling and you have enough wealth to take care of a big family, you have to make a plan, write it down, memorize it. Live by it, have a good relationship with God and your loved ones because you're going to need all the help you can get. Try not to be a follower, be your own man, focus never get addicted to any drug of any kind, read constantly, educate yourself and what you can create will be beyond perfect.

Guess what will happen after that, your vibe, your smarts and charisma will draw nothing but positivity around you. You'll have an abundance of luck, great friends and respect from your family. God on your side you'll have health, an endless amount of love. I mean think about it you know I'm telling the truth. You don't need to trust in any facebook schemes, Instagram ads telling you to invest in them and they can make you millions in a week but first if you pay Fifty-six dollars and i'll tell you the secret just give me all your information and bank card and you'll be in. Check out this four hour video and at the end you will find, get the fuck out of here.

Invest in yourself, open up things that will secure your future. Stocks, Bonds, life insurance, keep you a job to keep the cops off your back. Get you some college degrees under your belt and six figure jobs will be kicking down your door instead of you hoping and praying you get the job you damn well deserve.

All I'm saying is to take advantage of your youth, you really have all the time in the world to make your life better than your parents. Change your family dynamic and create a brighter future for your kids and there's without breaking any laws or gambling your way to the top.

My advice to an older man if you're reading this is to learn from your mistakes, go back to school it's never too late, be a better role model to your kids if you're not in their life and be a part of their upbringing they need your help. Any man that says they don't need their father in their lives is lying. Even if it's just conversations from time to time. He may not have been there for you financially or physically, maybe you can open a life insurance policy on him for his grandkids you never know unless you try. They say never let the wind close a door you left open. I repeat, get right with God, pray with your family. This new generation is so lost we have to get back to costumes. In New York we are so busy we can't even make it to church with our families but we can have church in our homes. We can teach the bible to our kids so they know God and have some form of family structure and values. We can make time to save our Family, even if you went to jail, even if the love of your life moved on, try not to be bitter. Put that bottle down, throw drugs down the toilet, there are too many agencies, shelters, counselors, programs out there that can help you help yourself. Never give up on life behind the bad choices you made.

Covenant House New York

Homeless Shelter 460 W 41st

Open 24 hours

Call (212) 613-0300

Call (988) Suicide & Crisis Lifeline

Alcohol and Drug Rehab - 30 Minutes from New York City

Call (866) 933-0474

I interviewed several women that are close to me on what the definition of a perfect man is, being that that is the true reason why I wrote this book. I wrote this book for the love i have for women and i want to have a blueprint for man to learn from so when he's ready to really go for his Queen he pretty much know what to look for, hell know what the vibes is, hell know how to give love and receive love, save himself a lot of time and heartache for him and his lady. As the muslims say, there's nothing like knowledge of self.

TABITHA

Here's a word from my close friend Tabitha when asked what is a perfect man to you;

There's no such thing as a perfect man and if there was that would be boring right? There would be no room for movement or growth together, However, to me, an Almost perfect man would be a man who has come to understand that his ego is not more important than the assurance he provides to his partner. Men who understand that pride matters when he's a provider and protector to his partner and not because he's the man in the relationship. Knowing that if he exercises his ear to listen and understand first, then to listen and respond with challenging his partner puts a dent of doubt that his partner can trust that even though he's the man in the relationship, he may not be the right man for her. He's also there to protect her from the inside out. Meaning her heart, her mind, her fears, her struggles. An almost perfect man knows that the true strength of a man to his women is providing her soul with safety and softness in his behavior towards her because women already know that physically a man is strong.

CHOCOLATE

Now a word from my friend Nae aka {Chocolate}

A perfect man is a man with strive, A man that could lead, A man with respect, a man that could reinsure his woman to make her feel like she is the best and the most beautifulest thing ever in this world. A man is protection, A man is Love, A man is the foundation i guess, The man is a provider, A man is a comforter that's what I think a perfect man is to me.

NAT

My Friend Nat kept it simple;

There's no Perfect man just like there is no Perfect woman!

Thank you, my lady!

SERVASIA

My little big cousin Servasia put it down for me;

Well, to me, no man could ever be perfect, but someone who shows confidence in himself, kindness to others, hard-working, respectful, is ambitious, supportive of his family, not just with money but in their dreams. Also a man who is willing to learn and grow. That's a perfect man to me.

Thanks cousin, you know I love you!

My Friend Gifty, Agyeman-siriboe Kissi says the perfect man does what I tell him to do! Has enough money for everything we need, respects his mother, makes time for his family, and always makes his women feel special.

My Cousin Melvenna Clark who I love to hear speak says No one in life is perfect, despite what we want everyone to believe Life is Life, it will never be perfect but exposing your true imperfect self opens you up to a world of deeper, meaningful and supportive relationships.

KAHLI

My young boy Kahli starts off, King!

The perfect man for starters according to what it means to be the perfect man is by training yourself how to be a man. For instance, humble yourself, take care of your own responsibilities, make things right not only for yourself but for someone you love and for someone that loves you. If you are in a relationship with the most beautifulest loving woman you know that loves you and thanks you dearly for what you do for her, meaning she cares for you and loves how you take care of her and yourself, it's a blessing to be with someone like that. A real man always makes sure he stays solid with a strong mindset, a man who doesn't give up but stands tall and strong like a warrior. A man will always keep his word and his promise to his woman/Queen. A man who will always keep it real and make things right not only for himself but for his family and his partner. A man must work hard to help himself build, grow stronger and must think positive and not negative. A man will always protect those who need him and they will surely do the same for him. A real man doesn't have the mind of a child and should never act like one. A real man acts like an adult taking care of all his responsibilities being truthful to himself and being good to others. Never have time for lies and cheating, never intentionally hurting someone or acting like a terrible person. A man will alway put God first and stay away from the devil following the path of light not darkness. Always showing leadership, never being a follower or a failure.

SHALIEK

A word from my God loving cousin Shaliek who I feel is a living prophet in my family and I quote, Look at the day, for it is life, The very Life of life in its brief course lies all the realities and varieties of existence, The bliss of Growth, the splendor of action, The glory of Power, for yesterday is but a dream, and tomorrow is only a vision, For today while lived makes every yesterday a dream of happiness and tomorrow a vision of hope. Look very well on the day and enjoy it because it's special. God will provide a perfect man everything he needs to survive and be Perfect. I hope to God the woman he is blessed to marry treats him like the King he is, Thanks cousin that was perfect. A true man of God, A lot of women don't even respect that anymore, they think it's lame especially this new generation, you can talk about God but you better be on your way to take them shopping or they don't want to hear about the Lord.

BOB MARLEY

Bob Marley was once asked if there was a perfect woman, He replies:

Who cares about perfection? Even the moon is not perfect, it's full of craters. The sea is incredibly beautiful, but salty and dark in its depths. The sky is always infinite, but often cloudy. So, everything that is beautiful isn't perfect, it's special. Therefore, every woman can be special to someone. Stop being "perfect", but try to be free and live, doing what you love, not wanting to impress others! Now That's Deep!

SHAQ

Shaq the black Aristotle says and I quote, "The older you get the more you realize how precious life is. You have no desire for drama, conflict or stress. You just want good friends, a cozy home, food on the table, and people who make you happy."

"You may not be a perfect person, but you are the perfect man for me and there's no one else I want but you." That's a good one!

"There is no such thing as a perfect man or a perfect marriage. But the one I have is absolutely perfect...for me." Now that's cute!

"The perfect man is the true partner, not a bed partner nor a fun partner, but a man who will shoulder burdens equally with you and possess that quality of joy," Whatever the hell that means!

"Money doesn't make a man. Muscles don't make a man. Tattoos don't make a man. Character is what makes a man! Let a man's character be his currency; that will tell you what he's really worth!"

A Perfect Man is Honest, takes care of his kids, gives up his seat to a woman, tells the worst truth instead of his beat lie, LISTENS! Reads, is well groomed, is secure enough to let her stand in the limelight, smiles, is romantic, minds his manners, holds doors open for others, is trustworthy and on time. Treats service personnel with the respect they are due, Loves and Respect his parents. May make mistakes but don't hold mistakes others make against them. Understands that he doesn't know everything. Makes a conscious effort to learn something new every day, loves hard, says what he feels and can read this without getting offended.

Read this to your son if you have one, do me that favor because what I'm trying to teach this new generation of man how to treat themselves and carry themselves like man. Something my father didn't have the chance to teach me and his father who passed when he was young couldn't teach him so I learned by watching other men such as my uncles and guys from my block. I always hang with older friends so I came to what I thought was a man real fast. I grew up hard and fast, my life could have gone in any direction. What I have learned the most is that life is about choices and learning from your mistakes because you're going to make them as long as you can learn from them you'll have a better chance at success. Learning is like repetition the more u do it the better moves you can make in this chess game of life. I don't talk much unless I'm drunk, being honest. I'm an observer first, I listen, then I talk which may make me seem like I know it all but I feel I just know how to read people and how I grew up. It was necessary to be that way, Who can you trust right!

What makes a perfect man in life?

The process of doing things regularly and achieving discipline can make a man perfect. Practice develops many good qualities in a person like hard work, discipline, tolerance, faith, willpower, dedication, determination, and confidence.

Jesus was called a perfect man. Did you know that Jesus spoke the truth, and the truth was eternal. History has no record of any other man leading a perfect life or doing everything in logical order. Jesus is the only person whose every action and whose utterance strikes a true note in the heart and mind of every man born of woman.

Does God see us as perfect?

The yes answer is based on Matthew 5:48

"Therefore you are to be perfect, as your heavenly father is perfect." Jesus was telling us that God is the standard against which everything else is measured.

That's why it's best that you have a better relationship with God first before any other. When your in trouble it's God help me, Stressed, God please, arguing with you girl it's God come take her now, even your woman pray right in front of you, Lord can you please remove me from all these troublesome people in my life, get them away from me Lord, WHO the HELL she talking about! Get you mad as ever but if you pray on it things seem to work themselves out and you end up moving all your stuff back in and that was all just a waste of time so you better start praying with your woman and your family, a-s-a-p! A family that prays together stays together and we lost that a long time ago, Tradition!

TRADITION

Tradition is a belief, principle or way of acting that people in a particular society or group have continued to follow for a long time. That's what we lost, when our grandparents passed i'm talking to the people over 40. Our Grandmothers we called them Big Momma she was the glue to the family and Church. When they went down or got too old the younger generations did not follow tradition. No Sunday dinners, no bible studies, no singing old slave songs, I mean church songs for hope and strength. I grew up in that crack epidemic in the 80's and I'm a witness of the abomination it caused to the black community. We really lost everything although our race survived it, our Tradition went up in smoke. It truly was a sad time in history that disrupted my entire family and many others. Now big mommas are little mommas, grandmothers are now 28 and husbands are younger than their wives. Men turning into women, women turning into men. Traditions are lost and all are going to Hell. I pray for the answers for this new generation of misfits. I leave it in God's hands and like they say it is what it is.

"Let him who without Sin cast out the first stone."

A perfect man is someone who doesn't care about all of that shizz on a girl. He's friendly, ambitious, kind, smart, witty, compassionate, righteous, judicious and a great conversationalist. He may not have the best features or the sharpest jawline. But he has a smile that makes you want to listen, eyes that tell you things would be ok. He's someone you can rely on. He's passionate about current affairs. He pushes you to do your best. He's your rock, your pillar of strength but he's also the guy who might refuse to help you once in a while because he wants you to stumble upon your hidden untapped reservoir of strength. He doesn't get intimidated by your accomplishments but revels in them.

DEAR MEN, let me tell you a secret…

WOMEN don't want a GOOD MAN until they are damaged. GOOD GUYS are never an option until a Woman is tired of being played, until a woman has kids with a guy that doesn't want anything to do with her, until she gets OLD, until she wants a husband.

Early in life, most women choose wrong guys, and then after those guys spit them out having used them, now they want a good man. The same good guy they thought was boring, The same good guy they didn't want to talk to.

Truth is good guys deal with damaged women, mentally, psychologically and emotionally. Bad guys get the best years…Good Guys deal with women with insecurities, women with anger and trauma. Don't get played, keep your head on a swivel and both eyes open. That's why I say let me update you when you start noticing certain behaviors from your women. Class Dismissed!

All lies right ladies, they say the one that truly loves you is the man that stayed in your life for years.That one guy friend that you probably never got physical with but thought about it. That dude you call brother but you sneak talk to him because your man doesn't trust you guys relationship. The one you let go, slip through your fingers, he may be on your mind as you're reading these lines. Yeah him! That's probably Mr Perfect but for some reason woman tend to fuck with who they like and not who they love. He's not popping enough or his money is always funny, his manhood isn't manly enough, he's cute but too chubby. Excuse after excuse and boom there goes the best thing that ever happened to you walking away because his feelings are hurt. That's never happened to me but I've heard stories.

I've Got one that I thought was crazy. A man has a wifey with two young kids, a boy and a girl about a year apart. He comes home one day early from work. Kids in school thinking this can be a perfect time to be with his lady, but instead he catches a guy on the coach with his wife, she sees him and screams out rape. The guy immediately starts to fight off his wife's attacker, runs for his gun and chases the dude off shooting his gun off in broad daylight missing every shot but saving his wife's life as the police come to the scene the wife explained that the attacker had been following her for days and he finally burst in her home and got what he was seeking, bad news for the hero her husband who gets hit with a loaded gun charge amongst five others. He goes to jail, calling his wife to get his family to make bail but no one has the money to help him out. He goes to trial finally with a bull crap appointed lawyer and gets ten years. Now he's pleading with his wife to send money and bring him his kids for a visit, she is not answering his calls, just straight ignoring him after all he did for her. Finally he gets ahold of one of his uncles on a call to his moms. Yo what's up with my wife, please someone go check on her and my kids she like ghosted me what's going on. Yo your mom went over there and caught her in your house with the dude you shot at, we didn't want to tell you she didn't get raped she was cheating.

And another one, man is down on his luck can't get work so him and his woman are arguing for weeks as the bills keep piling up and shes destroying this man ego from the inside out cursing him in front of his Kids, telling his mother he aint nothing, family trying to get him to leave her alone. One day she's had enough and tells him she's done with him, throws all his clothes out the house telling him she's talking to other guys she cant wait any longer for a better life. All this in the lobby of the projects. She let him kiss his kids good-bye. He pleaded with her that he couldn't live without her. He gave her the kids as they went on the elevator and the doors closed. BANG! Whole incident was recorded on the Lobby cameras and made the news.

I'm telling you these two scenarios not to scare you but to show you the power a woman can have over a man and vice- versa. The statistics shows that a lot of men are incarcerated at a young age over a woman, either there chasing money for them or there fighting over them, robbing or even killing. It's sad, men may be physically stronger but most women are mentally stronger and they can beat you in any court battle with one tear, I've seen it happen!

Jealousy is having y'all gossiping about someone you should be learning from!

That's the whole purpose of this book to let young readers know the best shot they have in life as a man to be Perfect for a woman and himself is to put God first, focus on finishing school before having kids and making sure you're mentally stable enough to handle what life has to offer you. Too much of anything could make you fail, drugs, alcohol, stress, fighting, eating, money, yes even too much money can drive you insane when enough is never enough and Love can be your demise you have to have a great self balance. I personally am going to start meditating. Writing for me is a vice, so is Music and cooking. It's fun to me to find myself, this person that God created in the light of himself. Peace is what I seek, love is what I give, and life is what I pray to be better everyday. Learning everyday not listening to people telling me who they think I am and what they think I should be or do, especially when I can see they don't have their shit together. I just laugh to myself and keep it moving. People seem to hate when you walk with God and move with peace and your attitude doesn't show your pain and what you've been thrown into.

They say never let them see you sweat. Be confident in yourself and strong, how you walk, how you talk the whole way you carry yourself. Stand for something or you will fall for anything. Women take notice of all that and they choose who fits them, even if you holla at them they already peeped your game and chose you. That's why they allow you to talk first and approach them. They still follow some traditions of letting a man speak first, buy the first drink or meal, ask them out on a date, get the digits unless you're super handsome to them then they are not shy to take the lead and be promiscuous.

People lie as well, you may be with someone else, married even. The devil is that strong to put you in the situations that test your will. Man or woman, that's when you really got to be right with God. I feel if you're out there playing relationship games it's got to be something you're missing at home. Maybe you are lacking in support, sex or even financially, something in you that has you seeking some other attention. You have to be strong and remember why you got into your immediate relationship in the first place. Rekindle your love by spending more time with one another, if that doesn't work then maybe it's time to split and look for your true calling in life. That's the funniest thing about life, you learn from your past to build a better future. No one can truly control your fate but a real man always has to be that because things can go left real quick

and you can easily lose everything you built faster then you can say, "Damn i fucked up!"

MEDITATION

Meditation is a practice in which an individual uses a technique such as mindfulness, or focusing the mind on a particular object, thought, or activity. To train attention and awareness, and achieve a mentally clear and emotionally calm and stable state. Meditation is practiced in numerous religious traditions. Since the 19th century, Asians meditative techniques have spread to other cultures where they have also found application in non-spiritual contexts, such as business and health.

PSYCHOLOGY

Psychology is always helpful, men never like to go see a psychologist. I don't think we can handle the truth when it's thrown in your face. Women love to kinda put you on the spot, play with your head and emotions. Love making things emotional, stress you out, that's their battle ground. Mind games, they fight with their minds and they fight to win.

Psychology is the study of mind and behavior. Its subject matter includes the behavior of humans and nonhumans, both conscious and unconscious phenomena, and mental processes such as thoughts, feeling, and motives.

Women are mostly the ones that suggest the use of a psychologist in the relationship due to their intuitive ability to process and express emotions clearer and finally have a greater desire to help others, often called nurture. This is evidenced in all the caring and teaching professions having larger percentages of women such as nursing, counseling, teachers, etc.

ROSIE

In the words of my friend Rosie (Deja), The Perfect man is so hard to think of because first what is perfection.What can we seek in a man that considers it to be perfect? Women are a different species that can never be satisfied, however if I had to build the perfect man my man would consist of Compassion, Teamwork and mental support but this goes both ways.

Masculinity is good however can be overpowering as women have become and evolved to be independent and strong as a man can be there through companionship and understanding. Love, wisdom, romance is key a lot of men in this day and age tend to forget the basic needs of romance, kisses, hugs, love, intimacy…etc

Common courtesy goes a long way. Well, at least my opinion of women in today's age needs constant reassurance as this generation is very promiscuous and experimental fidelity is the new "cool" now I can say for both sexes, having a side chick or side dude was a trend not too long ago. Men could have more love, compassion and reassurance. Women can show gratitude in return. In love with women the key is to be communicative, women love to talk and hear and listen, listening has to be key. A woman and man can't be together and not once have a real conversation just with a, hello and a cell phone in the face. We don't want that love anymore. We want to talk, go for walks, rap our favorite songs, dance, make funny jokes, and spend quality time with one another that is love. I always said,"anyone can be passionate but it takes true love to be silly." I follow that quote because being with a woman that's loving you understand that that's someone that is your safe, your home, not a come up or an object or a step stool but your energy, your bond, your story, real life.

Young man if you're on the right path keep doing what you're doing. We're all being judged by someone who isn't even close to having their life together. Stop setting yourself on fire to keep unworthy people warm. Wrong is wrong even if everyone does it. One small positive thought in the morning can change your whole day. Some people are so focused on bringing others down that they fail to realize it's that mentality that keeps them at the bottom. God gives gifts to everyone he created, find that gift, he will bless it and help you use it to touch many. What makes a gift great in God's service is not the magnitude of the gift. It is into whose hands the gift is given.

Personally, when I speak to people about the power of God, it is his gifts. God has blessed me with several gifts that I use to survive everyday. I tell people all the time to find your gift, that one thing that comes naturally to you, that thing that you do better than others. That is your gift, your super-power, if you put 110 percent into that gift you will not fail, it can make you wealthy beyond your dreams. Happier than you can ever imagine and so supportive that it may even help your children's children, children. Yes, that deep, life is about choices that is all. The better choices you make the better your future will be. So to these young men, become the backbone of this society again. Lets learn to make better choices early, better opportunities for our families, stay out of harm's way. By trying to listen to your elders who don't necessarily have to be a family member. Everyone you love may not have your best interest at heart. Read about successful people, talk to business owners in your neighbor-hood, watch positive people movements, talk to counselors in your schools, express yourself, tape in to your life and do not waste your time and no one else's

There are 100 ways you can kick start your future, what i'm telling you now i wish someone told me Get life insurance when you start working, invest in Stocks and Bonds. When you get some Capital invest in businesses, find out how much it cost to buy shares in them companies you spend a lot of your money in, Mcdonalds, White Castles, Starbucks, Chipotle yes you can invest as much money as you spend in these name brand companies that will set you up for life. Life is not easy, nothing is so if you're making fast money which may not have a good ending for you so i will never recommend selling drugs, boosting, or gambling. You go to jail and its game over you lose all your extra lives man, ain't no start over or reboot. The world will put you in a box like a toy and you will get old and dusty. Personally I love life too much to sit in someone's box, i'm going to do me and be free. I don't follow, and I don't give up, God wakes me up and I thank him for another day to go get it...

That's me, you find you, do you, no one can stop you but you. I'm far from perfect but I practice toward my perfection. I think of ways to be better, live longer, make more income, take care of the woman in my life, set up my kids when I go, I help people unconsciously and if you truly know me look me in my face and call me a liar, you can not. I deserve the best and I will get the best so help me God. He Gifted me with the ability to cook, Write and hustle. I use all these gifts to survive. Cooking pays my bills and I have been in the kitchen since I was six. Writing will God willing take care of my future and the hustle is the dedication I put into myself everyday to win. You have to take time to yourself, sit back and really be honest with yourself to learn who you are. Your strengths and weaknesses if you have a woman don't be scared to listen to her because they love to tell you that stuff. Then do your best to change your weakness and strengthen your talents if you can. If that doesn't work, change her. Hey im kidding but you only have one life right, make the best of it and jump on it earlier than later thats all im saying.

Put parameters in your children's lives and use strong standards to raise them. And start early, because it's a lot easier to build a child than it is to repair an adult. Words from my cousin Melvennia Clark. She's one of my gotos when I need to feed my brain. She's wise beyond her years and I love her for that, so yes I learn from women especially. The best ones help you win and I thank God that I have several on my team.

Things we should say to each other, You're so exquisite that I can't believe my eyes! You're an absolute treasure. I have to be honest…you're flawless. You're my ideal person–I idolize you.

When a man is honest and trustworthy, he instantly becomes appealing and desirable to a woman. If he's dependable, truthful, genuine, and speaks from the heart, he's a guy worth pursuing as people can take him at his word.

Women, on average, tend to be more attracted to men who have a relatively narrow waist, a V-shaped torso, wide chest and broad shoulders. Women also tend to be more attracted to men who are taller and older.

The ideal man also empowers his woman, it is a quality that defines an ideal man. He empowers his partner to grow by first understanding their needs. Secondly , he provides the necessary financial and moral support to accomplish this need. They also help with their everyday steps when they encounter hurdles.

How to talk to a woman you're interested in, be specific, compliment her on something that makes her special. Everyone loves to be flattered and she'll be pretty excited to hear what you have to say about her. If the feeling is mutual, she'll likely compliment you, too. Show her that you want her by politely asking for her number so you can reconnect at a later date depending on the circumstances. Ask her out so you can get to know her better, tell her your needs and wants then listen to hers. Try to get a deeper connection, tell her how you feel about her and what are your future plans with her in your life. Open doors, pull chairs, compliment her until she can't stop smiling. I don't know about sex on the first date, let's face it you're not me, but you may get a big kiss if you play your cards right.

It doesn't hurt to be a gentleman, but a woman can since if you're a gentle-man, please don't let that go over your head. So be a man about your approach and hopefully you may pull the women of your dreams. Here's the kicker though, that men seem to forget. Once you get her, the game doesn't change, you have to remind yourself daily of the things she asked of you, try to make every date like the first and everything should be A, OK.

LOYALTY

Loyalty implies a faithfulness that is steadfast in the face of any temptation to renounce, desert, or betray. Loyalty means being there for someone through the highs and the lows, and staying by their side regardless of the circumstances. Loyalty involves accepting and loving someone for who they are and not threatening to leave when things become challenging.

FAITH

Faith, the mind, the emotion, and the will Faith is an act of the whole man. This is where the three elements of faith that I just mentioned are understood. "Something that is believed especially with strong conviction." You gotta have faith in the world we are trying to live in today. Without it you will find yourself being scared to take a chance, with your feet in the ground you can't move but so much. Jump you may fall, but you also may land on your feet and take off running. Faith is reaching for the sky like they say, going all out for greatness just like what a perfect man seeks, Greatness!

DENZEL WASHINGTON

Denzel Hayes Washington Jr {born December 28, 1954) is an american actor, producer, and director. Known for his versatile work spanning over four decades of screen and stage, Washington has been regarded as one of the best actors of his generation, with The New York Times naming him the greatest actor of the 21st century in 2020. Washington has received a number of honors, including two Academy Awards, a Tony Award, two Golden Globe Awards, as well as the Cecil B. DeMille Award and AFI Life Achievement Award, and nominations for two Primetime Emmy Awards. That's all facts, now how's that for greatness for what we've known about Mr Washington.

What you may not know is that he was born in Mount Vernon, went to school at Fordham University for a BA in Drama and Journalism, Performed off-Broadway and even lived in the Bronx for a while. Washington bounced around to several schools studying his craft to perfection getting small rolls until he finally hit the big screen. All this before he met his wife Pauletta Pearson on the set of his first screen work, the television film Wilma, they married in 1983. Thereafter had four children, oldest son John David, {daughter} Katia, and youngest twins Malcolm and Olivia. He also has a twin brother of his own named David Washington

I can say to me Denzel is considered to be a perfect man because he did everything the right way. He's definitely receiving all his flowers alive and well and everyone looks up to him. I feel it's truly an honor to be in his presence. He's undoubtedly a man that you would love to soak up knowledge from when he's speaking. He's also a Capricorn like me, just thought I'd slide that in there to make myself feel good.

Denzel

"A miserable spirit can't stand being with a happy soul, remember that!

You may also want to look up Morgan J. Freeman who also received numerous accolades and has been acting since 1964.

Shelton Jackson "Spike Lee" His work has continually explored race relations, issues within the black community, the role of media in contemporary life, urban crime and poverty and other political issues.

Samuel Leroy Jackson, one of the most widely recognized actors of our generation, the films in which he appeared have collectively grossed over $27 billion worldwide, making him the highest-grossed actor of all time.

Those are a few men I look up to and admire their greatness. Men I would totally just shut my mouth and listen to them because I would get more Knowledge from them in one setting than reading twenty black history books.

BLACK HISTORY

Speaking of Black History, it's time for me to drop some gems on my future young men by mentioning names like Martin Luther King Jr, Malcolm Little, aka Malcolm X, Marcus Mosiah Garvey,Elijah Muhammed, Dick Gregory, James H. Cone, James L. Farmer,Jr, James Earl Jones. Read up on any of these men. They all made great sacrifices for our people, they gave us knowledge and power, some even lost their lives. Young men, you have to study the history of your people to have a sense of direction in your life. Naughty by Nature said no matter where you go there you are. Meaning no matter how far we've come as a people you have to know where you came from to know where you need to go in life. This applies to any and every race, each one has their own similar stories of struggle and triumph.

This generation doesn't know how to build healthy relationships. We end up saying things like "I don't owe anyone anything," but we do owe people something. You owe an apology to those you've offended. You owe gratitude to those who have supported you. And you owe respect to those you've disrespected. Accountability is a personal act of integrity and moral principles. We will continue to live in a broken society until we learn to take responsibility for our actions that negatively impact others.

People always rant about doing things all by themselves but forget when their moms were chastising them and they didn't want to listen. When their pops was disciplining them on how to run their life and they didn't consider his wisdom and counsel. Your grandparents taught you how to respect others and you didn't have any ears but quick to stand alone and turn your back on everyone that loves you and say i'm all alone in this world and no one loves me. Genes and DNA are so strong in humans I believe we were taught how to survive before we were even born. I mean think about it, you know you have to eat, sleep, go to the restroom, talk to communicate, walk to get where you need to be, move when you sense danger. We all are born with these spidey senses called Natural Instincts.

NATURAL INSTINCTS

Natural Instincts, human beings are driven by seven ancient instincts, or "primary-process affective systems,". These are seeking, anger, fear, panic-grief, care, pleasure/lust and play. The most powerful instinct is "seeking". We should be seeking God first and foremost. That's number one in my book, balance is very important for a man who seeks perfection in his life and purpose. Purpose is an abiding intention to achieve a long-term goal that is both personally meaningful and makes a positive mark on the world. When a man says I want to make my name mean something, that's his purpose. I'm sure he's pushing to do something great that will impact and change his whole family's life. Education is the gun and Knowledge is the bullet. The more education you get the stronger your name will be in this world. Your signature will be powerful; you can move mountains with a pen. Money, power, respect is the key to life. Money, power, respect all you need in life. The LOX and Lil Kim used their Hip Hop to stamp that in our brains and it's all facts. So please get your education, it's never too late. A million obstacles can get thrown in your way but one thing I know for sure is the more educated you are the more your intuitions and skills are worth to any company you apply to in any field that you are seeking to control for your financial growth.

You really never know what curve ball life is going to launch at you, practicing on being prepared to take your best crack at it wont hurt. You don't know who's going to come in and out of your life, life is not to be controlled, life is to be lived and everyday is a blessing from God. I'm learning, everyday I'm learning to be a better me. You have to learn yourself and be a better you, not just for your sake but for your family's sake as well. Think of yourself as a big piece of a puzzle and the puzzle will never be complete unless you plant yourself in your rightful spot. When you run from that connection your life will never be complete.

It's like mothers not talking to their daughters and sons who can't forgive their fathers. Siblings warring with each other, if you don't

forget and forgive your family puzzle will never be completed. You will never have eternal peace and a broken family hurts for generations.

PRESSURE

Pressure, continuous physical force exerted on or against an object by something in contact with it. A feeling of stress or anxiety because you have too much to do or because people are depending on you for something. A Perfect man has to be an expert on dealing with pressure. Pressure is strong enough to bust pipes, take down mountains and move planets. Not to get it twisted but women and men both have an extremely amount of pressure. That is one of our biggest arguments, who does the most in a relationship, who deals with the most stress, who works the hardest and goes through the most for the family. Do women win because they are women and more nurtured? Do men win because they have the option to run and opt out? Kids suffer and here comes the struggle, the race to fix what's broken. The desire to put that puzzle back together for the big picture, Family!

FAMILY, Isn't always about the people in your life who are blood relations.

It's about the people in your life who want you to be in theirs.

It's about the people in your life who accept you for who you are, support you in the things you choose to do and no matter what, are there for you.

It's the people in your life who love you, respect you and who you can depend on.

Unless you wear diapers, nobody can change you... Only you can change you!

Most women give men plenty of time to get their act together. Women don't give up easily in their relationships, they actually fight for those they believe in. However, most will not sit around for years (wasting years of their lives} for a man who will never change because he doesn't value her. Eventually she will come to terms that she is not the one for you and move on.

That's why as a man you have to learn how to take your time and pick your partner carefully. You can date and have sex without getting attached in a full fledged relationship. You have to be a man and like they say today,"stand on business," and tell the woman what her purpose is in your life. If it's just sex, friendship or business you're interested in being confident and straight forward always works. Let her decide what type of relationship she's willing to have with you and take it from there.

This tactic will help you grow stronger and know how to deal with different types of women. Teach you how to be a romantic and who to be stern with and who to buy flowers for, give gifts, show your sensitive side to. All women are not the same, some don't like soft men, they love bad boys. You can be both making you a woman magnet for sure. If you stay in shape, eat right and most importantly get your bread {money} up these women won't have a chance. A comedian named T.K. Kirkland said, 'if your name ain't on the lease, you're homeless.'

I took that as it's very important to get your own first and move the woman in with you then vice-versa. When women have too much power over a man they tend to use it no matter how much they say they love you, trust me your butt will be out on the street faster than you can say I only went to the store. Women get bored easily so if you're a man that doesn't make moves and you are lacking in the bedroom or financially that's a recipe for destruction and termination. So i will definitely advise you to get your own before you commit to something serious. Being a Perfect man is all about being empowered and ready for any and everything. Less chance of you getting cheated on and played with, I'm just saying.

Check your Goals,. his goal was clear to get accepted to Yale. Make a list of goals you would like to reach,

A higher degree, better job, business owner, new car, house, trip, cruise, land, anything that keeps you motivated for growth. Life goals are personal milestones that you're aiming to hit, and are usually bigger than everyday tasks and short-term objectives. No matter how difficult the goal is, if you reach it, it's a cause for celebration.

CELEBRATION

Celebration, a joyful occasion for special festivities to mark some event. Never ever be ashamed to celebrate, celebrating is a part of enjoying life to its fullest. Some people celebrate too much and go bankrupt trying to keep up with the Jones. All I see is athletes, actors, rappers on documentaries talking about how much money they blew when they got them big checks. People spend millions of dollars on birthdays and weddings, strip clubs etc... Going into debt to show off how much they got, to hide how much they don't got, wishing they can go back in time and do it all again. You cant really put a number on great memories if you got it, flaunt it so they say, but if you never had it and you waste it partying. You're a fool in my book and this is my book so yeah that's what I said, {Yea big Dummy}, in my Red Fox Voice.

SAVINGS

Savings, the portion of income not spent on current expenditures. In other words, it is the money set aside for future use not spent immediately. Saving money nowadays is the hardest thing to do. The economy is going out of whack, the cost of living, food, clothing is skyrocketing while the raises are set at a percentage not dollar amount. Meaning where getting 50 cent raises and the rent is going up 200 dollars. 100 dollars worth of food used to stretch out to 5 bags now it's only one. A pair of jeans is 2000 dollars and a pair of Jordans is going for the low low price of 1500 a foot. Yet and still you have to find a way to save something, watch your spending and partying. You must learn to prioritize and budget. If you know how much you're spending and get control of that, you can save a portion of what you're not, it's called survival. Tommorrows not promised so you really can't live like everyday's your last. Savings account, Life Insurance, 401K, Stocks & Bonds, Safes, Piggy Banks.

You may have to become a penny-pincher, tightwad, or even stingy. It's survival of the fittest when you're saving for your future.

I AIN'T GOT IT!

WILL

I'm going to explain the word Will in two short paragraphs.

Will, the desire, inclination, or choice of a person or group, The faculty of wishing, choosing, desiring, or intending.

A will provides for the distribution of certain property owned by you at the time of your death, and generally you may dispose of such property in any manner you choose.

Have you ever seen a movie where the family gathers in a room, like a den or library and the family lawyer pulls out some documents and reads them aloud then the family members start fighting because their father mostly has left the youngest child, the one he loved the most his whole estate. Then the older siblings go into a rag because they thought they deserved more than a lifetime of memories. Leaves his wife his car so she can drive off a cliff then surprisingly gives all his cash to the maid because that's who he was really loving in secrecy and had a bastard child with, named Hector. If you are laughing then you know what I'm insinuating. Mostly white people have accumulated enough wealth to have a will that gets orchestrated the right way. If black people have this blessing, they're lucky. I mean I've never seen it happen in my family, I hope I will be the first.

That's the First will, the second is Willpower

WILLPOWER

Willpower, a very strong determination to do something. He came into the hospital for help to quit smoking. By just willpower he failed to do so. A Perfect Man has to have willpower, he has to have the ability to continue doing something in the face of distractions, temptations, or adversity.

A man with willpower can take over the world. He's not scared to be a Boss and put people in their place like a chess game for one common goal, to win. You can conquer many things through sheer willpower. The CEO has it, it's a Godly feeling like a gambler that lets it ride. The will to win at any cost. You have to take risks, a leap of faith, try and try again to make your dreams come true. I will succeed, I will get rich, I will take good care of my family. You must speak it into existence, believe in yourself and your God given talents. Will your way to the top with your willpower. Listen to Nas I can for inspiration then you'll know exactly what I mean about willing your way to power.

HEALTH

Health is a state of complete physical, mental and social well-being and not merely the absence of disease or infirmity. Your health is one of the most important things in your life. You have to take steps to prevent illness and disease. Being proactive with your health means taking steps to improve your health before you get sick. Without your Health you will not have the power to do anything with your life, let alone accumulate wealth. So please go to the doctor at least every six months especially if you do drugs or are sexually active. It would be best to catch any sickness ahead of time so it could be cured God willing, if you die the game is over. Life is not a video game where you can power-up or get a free life pack running around in the streets. At the end of the day all you have is your health, it's worth more than diamonds and gold. You can get more money but you can't get your health back once it's gone so be very mindful and stay on top of that, VERY SERIOUS!

WEALTH

There's I'm getting money, I'm rich Biatch, and move Bitch get out the way, I'm WEALTHY!

Wealth is an abundance of valuable possessions or money, people buy Boats, Houses, and cars to display their wealth. Shaquille O' Neal is rich, the man that signs his checks is wealthy. Billionaire status so they say like Michael Jordan and Oprah Winfrey. You can get there with all the topics I just talked about. A million dollars was once a thing, now people, athletes, actors, rappers etc…won't sign anything for more than half a bill. It's amazing how much money they are giving out when people are dying for water and a pot of rice.

I'm very happy we have a lot of minority people that have accumulated Wealth, Will Smith, Jay Z, Beyonce, Martin Lawrence, Kevin Hart, Dr.Dre and many many more, have started from the bottom and turned nothing into some-thing. They are true living proof it can be done with willpower and a tremendous amount of hard work, deter-mination and Luck. Yes Luck they got lucky enough to have people come into their lives and help them fulfill their dreams. I always tell people it's all about the connections you make. Sort of like a Fraternity, a group of brothers that bounce ideas off one another and the best idea gets backed up 110 percent for one common goal of the group, Wealth. The perfect man gets his power from building a perfect team, get you a dominant team and you can get wealthy, IN GOD WE Trust!

Let money be thy servant, not master:

So, put thy wealth in use for mankind's sake:

Let progress come for fellowmen, faster:

What profits come if genuine, thou may take.

LUCK

Luck, success or failure apparently brought by chance rather than through one's own actions. Luck is a phenomenon and belief that defines the experience of improbable events, especially improbably positive or negative ones.

Luck is a bigger part of success than you think, but it can only take you so far. Luck is more important to career success than most people think. But talent and effort matter, too. The harder and smarter you work, the luckier you get. Lucky people are more likely to notice, create and act on opportunities. They use their gut feeling to make successful decisions. They persevere in the face of failure and take more calculated risks. They work to transform bad luck into good fortune by learning from experiences. A random occurrence that operates either for or against us.

Coincidence, is a random occurrence that brings two or more related incidents together. Something that's not planned or arranged but seems like it is. Technically, a coincidence is an occurrence of events that happen at the same time by total accident– like you and your man ending up at the same club on the same day at the same time.

It takes more than a lucky coincidence to be successful but it happens. Some people hit the lotto and don't look back. Others can win big at the casinos, some inherit their riches, causing the hard working retiring man to feel unlucky in life. It sucks to work for years to accumulate enough money to finally retire and it doesn't come close to a lucky man's good day. Punching a clock day in and day out while someone walks into a Bodega and walks out a millionaire in a matter of minutes. I'll take luck any day over that. How about you? I tell people all the time my kids took all my luck. I never find money anymore and if I'm moving late I usually have a bad day. I just leave everything up to God now, thanking him for another day, another opportunity to get up and go get it. He's my luck, if any money comes to me without tremendous hard work it's him. That's just my belief you can believe what you want. No psychic, palm reader or hypnotist can change me on that. They get paid to lie, I don't get paid to believe.

POLITE

Having or showing behavior that is respectful and considerate of other people is called being Polite. It takes nothing to be polite, some people blame their attitude on their upbringing and how well they get respected by others. This new generation has totally lost this insight, they don't carry bags, hold doors or give up their seats for the elderly like they used to. It's really a parent's job to teach their kids these skills before it's too late. If you encourage bad kids to be bad as a form of entertainment they most likely will be disrespectful in school and on the streets acting a fool for likes on Instagram, Tik Tok, Facebook. It may be funny but a disobedient kid is more than likely to grow up with a prison record or worse dead or in jail. Showing good manners towards others is called being nice. Nice refers to a characteristic of a person, Polite refers to the behavior of the person in interacting with others. A person that does not cause others uncomfort or pain is a "nice" person.

Don't get it twisted, I'm not talking about being a sucker, or letting people use you. I'm simply stating the facts on how society has taken a turn and grandparents are 28, parents are 16, no one has enough time to educate themselves, responsibility has come too soon. This dysfunction can be changed with education and awareness. Having awareness to know that something has to change or the cycle will continue. You have to break the bad patterns, set rules early, give your child duties to uphold and punishments if they don't obey you. Set a standard of living for them with love and respect and they will grow up leading better lives. Parenting is hard as shit even harder when you're doing it alone. Think about your life, your mistakes, what you were lacking and change that for your kids. Don't spoil them and give them too much more than what you had growing up. If you spoil your kid too much then they will depend on you as an adult and you don't want that. By the time they reach the age of ten they should be cleaning up behind themselves, doing laundry and lite cooking already. These skills will make them independent and eager to grow and have their own. The more your family grows, you should have more cars for you to drive. Keys to multiple homes and you should be loved and welcomed into any of your kids' homes more respected than their wives and husbands if you raised them with dignity.

If you're reading this and shaking your head you know I'm telling the truth and only the truth so help me God!

BALANCE

Balance is the physical steadiness that keeps you on your feet. In everyday terms the word balance means to give several things equal amounts of importance, time, or money so that a situation is successful. Balance can also be mental steadiness or emotional stability.

It took me years to learn how to balance my life and I still don't have it 100 percent. I'm such a lovable guy everyone in my family requested their own individual time. I had to work, get rest and occasionally go to the gym to get through the week but that's personal time. My wife had a list of duties for me to do as well as my kids needing to hang with me in the park, play video games or go out to eat dinner. My wife gets at me about all the things she has to deal with but she vaguely forgets that I have to deal with her and the things she's dealing with while taking blamed for half of it, then later on dealing with all of it, so she could love me again, now that's a crazy deal.

You have to be a G and take your punches like a man, never let them see you sweat or run from diversity that may change your life. Good or bad if change awaits you in the future make sure that you are in total control of the situation. You move when you're ready and be a man of your word. I balanced my life by giving everyone a day including myself. I work nights Saturday thru tuesday, Wednesday is for wifey, Thursday the kids and friday is for me to do the things i like to do, get sleep hopefully then i'm back to work Saturday beginning my weeks cycle,

Believe you me, lines get crossed sometimes so I have to keep my balance like I'm riding a skateboard down a steep hill and I don't want to hit a rock, scrape up my whole left side just to prove that I can be Superman and do everything my family needs.

STRUCTURE

Structure, fitting together, building, although it's certainly used to describe buildings, it can do more than that. A family's structure includes the relationship of its members, your body structure can refer to how your muscles and bones fit together. It's an arrangement, anything that has been put together in an organized, deliberate way can be described as structured.

Kids need it the most, if you raise your kids with structure they will be the most organized people you know when they become adults. You don't have to worry about them being a menace to society, living all confused and can't make it without you helping them.They can manage their credit and take care of their bills, maintain a household with kids and make you proud.

GYM

Gym, physical Therapy, great for mind, body and soul. A gym is a public place where exercises are practiced. The preferred way to dress at a gym these days is in shorts or sweatpants, but back in Ancient Greece, men commonly exercised naked, i never knew this, not today we dont get down like that in 2024, but thankful that Greece created this space and mindset. Working out is very important. It helps you focus and have a great amount of energy to get a lot of things accomplished. Exercise can improve your mood. Help you sleep better, and reduce your risk of depression. You can maintain a healthy body weight and focus.

Start slowly and build up gradually. Give yourself plenty of time to warm up and cool down with easy walking and gentle stretching. Then speed up to a pace you can keep doing for 5 to 10 minutes without getting overly tired. As your energy improves, slowly add to the amount of time you exercise.

The Perfect Man looks forward to this self time to create a better self, making himself more attractive to women. Working out and getting buff really helps your confidence. Self confidence is what attracts women, some guys are naturally self confident. Some need an expensive car and clothes, others need muscles to make them feel relevant. It attracts women no doubt, even the ones you dont even want.

To be a Perfect man you must have some type of physical masculinity or your finances better be on point. Your drive has to be right and your crib must be comfortable. Sad but this is how women rate their future husband. It's true, smell and look like a bag of money and you can have any woman you want. The pick of the litter so they say, you may have a handful of women that stand on their own two, may even take care of you for 6 months to a year. After that you better be ready for Sir you need to find a job. You can put it down all you want, Money wins, stability tops all and I can do bad by myself will come into play. Most women hate being the breadwinner but they love running the household. That's kinda the way relationships are structured. The old man in the field, woman in the house format that went on for generations.

These independent new generation women on the other hand are making it hard for the Perfect man to be dominant, but they'll find a way, A man is just a man and look at us, you'll love us, OH stop it!

NUTRITION

Nutrition is the study of food and how it affects the health and growth of the body. Nutrients are substances found in food that our bodies use to grow. Men have specific nutritional needs, and a healthy diet can help them maintain good health. An unhealthy diet can increase the risk of chronic diseases like cardiovascular disease and type 2 diabetes, as well as mental health issues like anxiety and depression. Being overweight or obese can also increase the risk of heart disease, stroke, some cancers, and mental health problems, and can decrease male fertility.

Geez, what we put in our bodies is extremely important, but like me and a lot of other people I know who grew up with an overwhelming amount of stress tend to go straight to food for comfort. Depression at a young age is so common nowadays. If you're suffering from anything, please speak up and get some help from a family member, priest, counselor, teacher, best friend, anyone you can trust with your personal information and your feelings. Please the world needs your wisdom and energy so dont think to harm yourself or others if your going through something help is the easiest thing to ask for. You'd be surprised how many people will come to your aid. Even if you're dealing with the loss of a loved one, the more you talk about them or any situation the heart could cope better and ease the pain. Taik, write, workout, lean on your friends and family. That's what they're there for, they want to know your business anyway. If you keep things to yourself, you really cant cry and say no one's there for you when you yourself are not trying to let no one in.

Treat yourself, don't cheat yourself, try to stay away from bad fatty foods and sodas. You are supposed to drink 8 glasses of water a day even though I'm a work in progress. I work to better myself everyday, it's tough but the end result is a Perfect healthy man that can give 110 percent to a better life for everyone around him.

Are you that Perfect man? Ladies, you think you can teach your sons these tools to be a Perfect Man, I think you can, any and everything is possible thru Christ, family, and love.

COMMUNICATION

Communication is the sending and receiving of information and can be one-on-one or between groups of people, and can be face-to-face or through communication devices.

Four types of communication are verbal, non-verbal, visual and written communication. No matter how we communicate, start by thinking about what the reader/listener should think, feel and do once they've heard or read our message.

Effective communication is the process 0f exchanging ideas, thoughts, opinions, knowledge, and data so that the message is received and understood with clarity and purpose.

Communication in a relationship is the key to a great one. First off before you start talking out your butt, you must understand your feelings before you can express your feelings, you have to know what they are. Be discerning about who you share with, Respond, don't react, find the right time to talk, be direct and pay attention to body language and tone of voice. Most importantly be a good listener, if you don't listen you cant hear what's being said to you to understand. People can feel a one sided conversation and tend to stop talking. When a man becomes quiet and distant that means he's with someone that he cant express his emotions with, men have feelings too. They can be hurt when they feel disrespected, it's not just women who get abused in a relationship. Men get uncomfortable, stressed, and we even cry. Love makes us vulnerable as well, we get cheated on physically abused, mentally and verbally just like women do, then on top of that we get called soft if we express any emotion other than manly. So we really gotta be careful who we let our guards down to. Most men express themselves around their mothers, your woman won't understand you like your mother so if you're a man and you have your mother in your life alive and well appreciate her to the fullest her ears will never be closed to her son, good or bad.

EMPATHY

Talk about what you want, need and feel, I need, I want, I feel, accept responsibility for your own feelings. Listen to your partner. Put aside your own thoughts for the time being and try to understand their intentions, feelings, needs and wants {this is called empathy}

Empathy means expressing someone else's feelings. It requires an emotional component of really feeling what the other person is feeling.

An empathetic person values others feelings enough to let them explain themselves, even when it's uncomfortable. If someone confronts you about something you did to them. Its important to listen and ask questions rather than react defensively. That's how most altercations happen, no one shows empathy and care, so a fight may result in ending a great friendship or relationship. You have to be patient, Listen, and understand each other's point of views. It's perfectly fine to agree to disagree but not listening may cause a big problem and a hard head makes a soft behind every time.

SYMPATHY

Sympathy, on the other hand, means understanding someone else's suffering. A sense of compassion, it's when you feel bad for someone else who's going through something hard. The ability to feel sympathy for others is a great part of what makes us human, and it's what compels us to reach out and offer help.

I have a big heart so people may label me as being too sympathetic, I care about my people so some may take advantage of that. The funny thing is the people that use me the most love to tell me to watch out for others, that's so ironic. I'm just the type that spreads love and if it's not always reciprocated I'm good with knowing I helped someone today and God knows my journey. So i'm not a sucka i just care about others' well being. Not a killer but dont push me as the saying goes. I guess the things that happen in your life mold the person you are today. I was taught the value of family love at a young age and everyone can feel my presence on that matter. Others were raised differently but I totally understand all and I can't change who I am for what you want me to be. I can't do you like you did me. I need all my blessings.

Be around people that inspire you and lift you up. Sometimes your worst enemy can be yourself. You'll need to reprogram your brain with positive ideas and thoughts to replace the negative ones.

Ideas don't work unless you work!

You don't always have to be strong. Sometimes you need to scream, cuss, throw shit, or have a really good cry. But you always, always, always, need to pull yourself back together, then go back to being the badass you were meant to be.

Don't 'fake it until you make it,' Face it until you make it. Get up. Work hard, fail. Stand back up, face it again. Do it a little better, fail again, get back up, Repeat.

People assume your kindness and the smile you wear must be from an easy life.They don't know I walked through darkness alone and turned my pain into power. My wounds into wisdom. The mistreatments by others into boundaries, and generational curses into blessings. I just chose not to let the worst define the best of me that's yet to come.

Never judge a person for how they handled a type of pain you never felt. Biggest lesson is don't ever think it can't happen to you or someone you know and love. You must learn to be humble and give God the Glory he deserves from you.

These are what I call words to live by, I get a lot of these messages from my friends and loved ones, you see I put people around me that want to see me win and I them. Aint no I in team but there's an me in it no doubt. That's the worst problem we have is thinking about ourselves. We must crawl out of that crab barrow leaving everyone else behind. Not thinking once we get out go get a damn ladder. I didn't let you stand on my back so you could make it and don't look back. I believe God gave me the strength and wisdom to create this book to uplift a new generation of men that can do better, think better, and carry themselves higher than they ever thought imaginable. I'm almost 50 years old and I'm still learning to this day. To be a perfect man you have to be a man that strives for perfection. I believe a person that comes from nothing deserves everything. If you move with that mentality no one can pop a cloud in your dreams. You'll wake up everyday with drive and vigor. No, will be the new,Yes and time will be like counting money in a bank, Costly!

ATTIRE

Attire, A formal way to say "outfit," Casual dress includes items like T-shirts, button-down shirts, blouses and sweaters on top. Bottoms might include jeans, khakis, linen pants, cropped pants or shorts. Casual shoes can include sneakers, loafers, low heels or sandals.

I don't think jeans are an appropriate attire for a wedding, that is why my closet has something for every occasion. I can dress up-down street or business. Your wardrobe is very important to a Perfect Man. He must keep up and move with the times, with a style of his own that fits him like the king that he is. Clothes make the man, I feel you can walk through any door with the right attire. Women and men will take notice when you command a room. The more money you make the better your attire should look and the farther you will go. People sleep on clothes, they are the biggest confidence booster before cars and homes. Your smell game complements the attire and the attire complements the lifestyle.

Suits are an essential part of a man's wardrobe. Whether for formal occasions or everyday wear, it can show a unique style and taste. A well cut suit makes every moment confident and easy.

A Perfect man must have clothing etiquettes, knowing what is appropriate to wear for particular occasions. What you wear is defined by the entertainment. Clothes that are fit to be seen, presentable and respectable. Way different from Apparel which is a broader term for all clothing, shoes, bags, jewelry, accessories etc. "Man makes the money, money never makes the man," says Jay-Z who got plenty, Respectfully! Another man I admire that started from the bottom doing what he had to do to get what he got. Proving that anything is possible. If you stay grounded and keep swinging you too can be the next rap,superstar mogul.

No matter the fit you must be prepared to let the people know who you are, what you stand for and where you come from. The perfect attire will definitely accommodate that for sure.

GENTLEMAN

Gentleman, a true gentleman is emotionally mature, mentally sharp, informed, and not ashamed to ask for help.

A gentleman embraces civility by valuing all people and treating everyone with respect. From the janitor to the CEO, he carefully considers how his behavior and words impact others.

Being a gentleman doesn't just mean being polite and courteous to women, it means being respectful to other men, to the elderly, and even to children. A true gentleman shouldn't be able to turn his charm off and he should be kind and respectful to absolutely everyone who deserves it.

This is one of the main things these kids in this new generation are lacking. How to be respectful, I've seen disrespect to the highest level in these streets. Kids especially these young men are smoking weed around babies, punching out old men out, they cant even hold an elevator for an old lady in a

Wheelchair or help with bags anymore. That proves to me that this group is lost and there's no hope for the future which will get worse if we don't take notice and catch it quick and fast. I held a train door for a lady the other day and she screamed out, Thanks , Chivalry is not dead, somebody must've raised you right. I thanked her and laughed then helped her to an open seat some guy was about to knock us over for. All I could do was look and shake my head. It hurts me to see how the world is changing. No one cares anymore, my sister told my wife one time that she got the last great guy, I thought she just said that because she loved me but I see what she meant. I can't help myself, right is right,and wrong is wrong. I'm just glad I haven't seen a man beat a woman in public yet. I'll probably blow my top and be on the news with him, Lord knows!

GROOMING

Grooming, maintaining personal body hygiene to look healthy and presentable. To appear well groomed these topics must become second nature to you, shower daily, hair care, dress appropriately, exercise regularly, protect yourself from sun, healthy teeth and gums. These tactics will create a Perfect Man appearance every time you look in the mirror or step out in public. No one can doubt your swag and you will stand out in a crowd. Women will give you their number without you asking. Doors will open for you that you will not believe just by getting "Flee," that's what they say right, you looking," Flee."

ORGANIZE

Organize, able to plan things carefully, keep things tidy, and work effectively. Young man please focus on what's important. Remind yourself of your long-term goals and revise them when necessary. Make lists of different objectives you need to remember, manage your time well, use calendars and planners, Delegate tasks, manage your mail and phone calls, reduce clutter, and stay organized. These tactics will help you become an organized person. Orderly and efficient, an excellent time manager. My aunt told me this when I was young and it stuck with me to this day. She said it's better to be early than late, and it's better to be late than absent. If you're late then you can catch up on what the lesson is, if you're absent you're lost, you didn't hear the lesson at all so if you're tested you have a better chance of failing because you didn't receive all the information to pass.

SCHOOL

School is definitely the blueprint to a successful work life. It teaches you how to get up early and be on time. Gives you organizing skills, communication skills, rules and regulations to life and work. Programs us to be a Boss or fall in line and be cubical punch the clock employees. The better you organize yourself for success the easier it is to become just that. Businesses love people that are neat and dedicated to their job, you can tell a slacker from a mile away. They are always late and complaining about the easiest tasks, always thirsty for breaks, never really focused and always talking about quitting and how much more their time is worth than yours. They're obviously working a job they dont love or planned to do as a child and if their life was more organized they would have put themselves in a position to win doin what they love and making easy money. If you love what you do then it doesn't feel like work at all. You'll look forward to what your job is and you will thrive in that field taking great care of yourself and the family you're grinding for.

CALENDER

A chart or series of pages showing the days, weeks, and months of a particular year, or giving particular seasonal information is called a calendar.. Mastering the calendar is like mastering time which is very important. If you can master your time you can master your business and money. You can use it to calculate your funds, know when you have to dish out money or when you can save, budget yourself, the key to organizing your life is easy when you master your time and your calendar.

FRIENDSHIP

Friendship, A relationship of mutual affection between people. It is a stronger form of interpersonal bond than an "acquaintance" or an 'association", such as a classmate, neighbor, co-worker, or colleague. A state of enduring affection, esteem, intimacy, and trust between two people.

True friendship may be defined as mutual unconditional love. This can be a different type of love than you might receive from your family or your partner. A true friend cares about you and is able to have concern and respect for your thoughts and emotions even when they may not agree. If the disappointment you are experiencing in a friendship has become consistent, it may be time to redefine your definition of a true friend.

I have a million friends but a handful that has my heart and trust. My moms was number one, the only one I can keep my deep dark secrets with and I know no one will repeat it back to me or throw things in my face. If they knew how I really felt about them. Everyone is not built to fit in your life, real friends never leave no matter how long you haven't spoken or spent time together. They know and understand you so even if life splits you up when you see each other again it's like you never spent time apart. I think God for these friends because when they are tested they always pass with flying colors. They never judge you and are always happy to see you again. I missed all the ones that passed and I always figured out a way to make it right and mend any lost time or problems that were acquired in our relationship. I don't think you can ever truly hurt a true friend. They stay solid to the death, ride or die. I love them so much it's funny because a true friend loves to pull cards on who they think is phony in your life and be ready to come to blows to prove it, it's crazy. Respect to all my true friends I call my brothers and sisters even though we have a different type of blood. Some friends are even closer than family due to their consistency and how they show their love in abundance.

Friends, "how many of us have them?" Thanks, Whodini.

WORK

Work, business, occupation, industry, employment. Work is an activity that a person engages in regularly to earn a livelihood. Earning one's livelihood is very important to keep food in your belly and the clothes on your back. You need to keep a substantial amount of income to take care of your family. Even more if kids are into play. The Perfect Man can cover all bases and build revenue, enough to support everyone he loves. He's Grand kids, kids could eat, he's like a no-limit soldier and there's no limit to the heights he could reach.

I truly believe schooling is the best tactic, the more you know, the more your knowledge is worth. I also believe self employment is the best route. It leaves out any middle man and you alone receive all the Capital. It takes a lot of work to start from the bottom and work your way up. "Started from the bottom now we here," indeed. You know what you put into your business and how hard you worked when you go to the bank and your zeros look like you hit the lottery. Whoever reading this right now wishes they could be in that position. They say money is the root to all evil, I say if you got it you can pay evil to get the hell out your way. You can work for a company just try to make sure you're the top dog with the highest pay. More money means more responsibility and risks but that's why you gotta stay fit and protect your mind. That's what they are paying for, be that money making machine that can take that company to the next level, for generations to come. Another smart move would be to employ your family and they don't have to have the best positions but this will keep them out of your pocket and strengthen the family. We didn't send you to college for nothing, Junior, show some love.

I worked at a job for 24 years and I'm still not wealthy. That's because I didn't get the schooling I'm telling you about. Please parents, if you're in your kids' life, encourage them to go to school. That should be their first priority, especially if you couldn't due to raising them they owe you that much. Give them goals to reach to keep their minds growing and learning. A household full of drugs, arguing, and partying is getting old. You can do it, just show your kids a little more respect as they grow watching you as their mentor and guardians before it's too late. Remember that old saying I want my kids to be better than me, you gotta push for that 110 percent. The younger you structure them the better this will go for you and your family.

LIFE INSURANCE

Life insurance can be defined as a contract between an insurance policy holder and an insurance company, where the insurer promises to pay a sum of money in exchange for a premium, upon the death of an insured person or after a set period of time. Life insurance covers the insured person's life. So if you pass away while your policy is active, your beneficiaries can use the payout to cover whatever they choose- medical bills, funeral costs, education, loans, day-to-day costs, and even savings. While life insurance is often thought of as something you leave to your beneficiaries after you have died, there are ways you can use your life insurance while you're alive. This can be used to pay down debt, make mortgage payments or simply to help finance major expenses. But not every policy allows you early access so do your homework and choose wisely.

The different types of life insurance, Term, Whole, Universal, Burial. Survivorship, Mortgage, and Supplement. Research and learning the different insurances is very beneficial to your future, family name, and legacy. I learned a lot about it when my mother and father passed in 2018. I had a policy on my moms for years for 50k. When she passed and my family got together for the funeral arrangements my aunt looked over to me and asked if I had life insurance for my mother. I was distorted and couldn't remember if it was still active, I think I was still in shock but I said yes. We called it in and i ended up paying for my moms expenses which was an honor for me because as much as i didn't want her to go i was happy i could afford her burial without leaning on my family, so i was proud for that, i prayed and thanked my mother for filling out the paperwork with me. She was happy her son had her taken care of and she didn't have to be a burden on me and my sisters. I know you watching me lady, we love and miss you thats a fact. Thank you! Now back to the book!

My father on the other hand was a product of the State, He was incarcerated at the time of his passing so my Aunts bonded together to cover him. God bless my ladies man, they mean the world to me, just amazing women. I owe them the world but that's another novel in itself one day. I told y'all my testimony to show you how life insurance worked for me and mine to this day. I got 2 open policies for my 3 kids to split and one personal one to bury me so my family won't have that debt to cover because caskets costs, trust me I know.

HEALTH BENEFITS

Health Benefits is a contract that requires your health insurer to pay some or all of your healthcare costs in exchange for a premium. Health insurance is a legal entitlement to payment or reimbursement for your health care costs, generally under a contract with a health insurance company. Health insurance provides important financial protection in case you have an accident or sickness.

There are many types of insurance policies, Life, health, homeowners, and auto are among the most common forms of insurance. Unfortunately there is no universal healthcare. The U,S, government does not provide health benefits to citizens or visitors. Any time you get medical care, someone has to pay for it, unless you move to Canada they have free Health coverage.

Health insurance can help protect you from the high costs of illness or injury. It also helps you get regular health care, such as exams, preventive care and vaccines, medications, and therapy which can cost a lot. That's why it's very important to get coverage for you and your family. Some jobs cover your health insurance taking a percentage from your check, you can go to a hospital insurance office or Google insurance on your phone and order it directly. It can cost as much as a car payment so you have to get your money up to afford it. Do your homework to find cheaper ones but at the end of the day it's a must have that can save your life. Something you'd wish you had when needed because life is unpredictable and anything is possible at any given time.

Due to rising health care costs the unprivileged, blacks, and hispanics having the highest percentile have a much greater risk of accumulating medical bills that you may not be able to pay. In a worst-case scenario, you could be sued and have your wages garnished.

BILLS

Bills, an amount of money owed for goods supplied or services rendered, set out in a printed or written statement of charges. Like an invoice, a bill outlines how much money a customer owes a business. Bills are important but extremely hard to stay on top of, the more your family grows the more your bills will accumulate. The most critical bills for me is, Rent, Food costs, and Electricity. Other bills we choose to build that are not really a necessity, I call them luxury bills are, Automobiles which include Car Insurance, Cabletelevision, and that all Mighty Cell Phone. These bills are more needs then wants, you don't need them to live but you do want them to get by. My Ghost bills as I call them are, Going out to eat, drugs unfortunately this includes Liquor, cigarettes, weed ect…And the one everyone sleeps on but you file it in your taxes if your smart that God bless it, Transportation, Trains, Buses, cabs and now them new scooty bikes.

The only ones that don't have to worry about bills are children. They just frolic and have fun while the adults walk around in a daze scratching their heads living from check to check making ends meet especially if you're a single parent and all the pressure is on you. Trying to raise a Perfect Man then this book is definitely for you and yours. Having a drink wishing you were a kid again doesn't help, just a coping mechanism that gets you by for the moment to ease your mind and get your thoughts off your problems. Some do that,others jog or go to the gym and exercise anything to woosah and take the edge off of this tuff life.

The crazy thing is you're gonna die owing bills so you have to get control of your finances, be an adult, organize your businesses, check your needs and wants, lower your cost by controlling your spending.habits. Minorities have it the worst because we've suffered so much in this country to get to where we are. We live like everyday is our last. We buy expensive things and treat ourselves to the best of things every week causing us to go into debt quicker than a Kentucky Derby Horse Race. You know why billionaires stay rich because they dress like bums and eat like rabbits. No judgment, I just watch people closely. That's how I learned, that's how I survived. You as a Perfect Man must do the same, learn to listen and understand quickly for the win.

NEEDS AND WANTS

Needs and wants are an important part of an economy. Needs are things that people require to survive. Food, water, clothing, and shelter are all needs. If a human body does not have those things, the body cannot function and will die. Wants are things that a person would like to have but are not needed for survival. Money is definitely a need, whether you're saving for emergencies, paying off debt, or building retirement savings, all financial goals can be considered needs. Achieving your Money milestone is essential to staying financially fit and takes precedence over your wants throughout your journey to financial Freedom.

Food, water, clothing, and shelter are all needs. If a human body does not have those things, the body cannot function and will die. Wants are things that a person would like to have but are not needed for survival. A want may include a toy, expensive shoes, or most recent electronics.

We can classify wants into three broad categories in economics. These are Necessaries, Comforts, and Luxuries.

Happiness is the biggest challenge, not knowing what you want in life brings fear for your future, confusion, that causes unhappiness and stress. Money is the most necessary, not having enough of it and the time to accomplish the things you want to do brings on frustration. It's valuable to you to put a great support team around you and your family. Freedom, Peace, Joy, Balance, Fulfillment, and Confidence are keywords to a self rounded human being. Im just spitting the facts to guide these young men who have to one day be the protectors of this world.

WOMAN

Woman, an adult female human being, that can bear offspring or produce eggs. Let's face the facts here a man can't do any two of these things.This is a gift from God to help this planet evolve. All females can reproduce human, or mammal for new life on earth. That's why men were programmed from birth to protect.

I have 2 little sisters and I can remember my mother as tough as she was telling me to help her, help me with your sister this, carry that, go to the store we need this. It was a part of my upbringing. My Grandmother, my aunts, "Boo" my nickname from my father stuck with me for life. Boo we need you to be a strong man. Boo, you the man! All programming to make me a protector of women. That's the training, the grooming, the blueprint that's being lost in today's society. It went from protecting women and children into protecting yourself, it's all about you, nobody cares about me but me, I dont give a shit about no one. These young men have been brainwashed, let out and hung out to dry. I feel it's the government killing all the programs that bring togetherness, care, and companionship. They stopped music, and art, limited after school programs and closed down the centers that teach physical ed and sports. Self defiance classes, mentorship, and counseling.

I think they are trying to wipe us out by pumping money into Liquor stores, drugs and legalizing weapons. KRS ONE said we headed for 'Self Destruction' and he was right. It's all in the 90's music. I don't know what this 2020 stuff is teaching but these kids are as good as lost. With everyone into themselves humanity is dying at a meteor rate. No one wants to learn, a handful wants to read, but everyone wants to win and pray for a bag full of money to fall in their laps to be greedy and blow. We risk our livelihood for it our freedom and our Life.

PRISON

Prison, A state of confinement of captivity, a place not to be glorified for what the government considers to be lawbreakers. An institution far from higher learning or rehabilitation. Confinement for a person convicted of serious crimes. Jails typically house people awaiting trial and those serving short sentences, while prison confine convicts long term.

If you hear anyone talking about the Clink, glasshouse, gaol, slammer or penitentiary be very aware that they take chances in life you may not be willing to be a part of. No one can force you to do a crime but they can build a fantasy in your mind to make you join them to succeed in it. The goal is always to get a bag of money. People that live fast and dangerous are not ones who like to work hard for slow money. They take risks and are not scared to go to jail or die for their cause. They are selfish and don't care about the damage they bring to their family and friends. You can be friends with a criminal if you're from the hood but make some boundaries and let them know where you stand in their lives. I have plenty of family members that've been in prison, a lot of friends too. I stayed out of trouble by keeping busy working and schooling. My father did Life in prison and died so i've never been a fan of jail and the system. I don't interact with police unless they force me and I don't tell authorities on my peoples from how I was raised in the Bronx, no snitching street rule number 1.

The Perfect Man should stay far from trouble. You don't want to sit in a nobody's prison away from your family, not being productive, wasting the life God gave you eating crap and smelling other men's feces while they watch you shower contemplating your death because they're bored and want a bigger rep, what a Life! One thing I wont ever do is glorify prison and wish death or incarceration that don't help anyone reform. They just die or come out more misunderstood than ever. It'll take you years to fit back into society let alone make up for the damage you did to your family, just a big mess when you go the wrong route so do yourself a favor and don't.

CONFUCIUS

Confucius, a Chinese philosopher, says that "a perfect man is highly value-minded and does not follow any one. He is modest in words because he knows that people may make distortions easily in their speech. He is a man of action not words. A perfect man searches for everything in himself while an inferior man searches what he wants in others. Faithfulness, dependability, kindness (67% of women said they find it a turn on), moral integrity, fatherliness(defined as patience and caring and desire to be a dad).

A perfect man would never act from a sense of duty: he'd always want the right thing more than the wrong one. Practice makes a man perfect. Continuous practice in any subject to learn anything. There is no alternative to hard work and success; we must have to practice in the particular field on a regular basis in which we want to succeed. Boxers, Athletes, Singers, all practice. Dancers, Actors, even Artists have to paint for years before they start making Masterpieces. Bruce Lee, one of my favorite fighters, practiced Wing chun gung Fu martial arts daily. Sometimes, multiple times per day. He mostly self-taught himself from reading books, watching films, and training with others and sparring. They say he died from taking a headache medicine that gave him a swelling in the brain. Some say he got poisoned because he was becoming unbeatable. He practiced his technique so much it created a new style that his elders wouldn't allow. He was going against traditions and making a lot of enemies.

I am not a Perfect Man by far, I'm just trying to give some key steps to becoming one for my misguided youth who I feel are lost. Lost in the system, disconnected from their families and don't know their place in this world. Being perfect is becoming a better human being. What's wrong with eating right and getting into shape? What's wrong with grooming yourself and being polite to the elderly? What's wrong with getting an education and making top pay so you can live a life with no worries without being a criminal? what's wrong with

Staying your butt out of jail and not hurting your family who need you? If your thought is nothing then this Book is working on you. Opening up your mind for a better you to come.

Come on no more excuses, do better, be better, make your name mean something your family could be proud of. Legacy, your legacy is something that is passed on. But

Legacy can take many forms. A Legacy may be one's faith, ethics and core values. A Legacy may be monetary or your assets. A Legacy may come from one's character, reputation and the life you lead- setting an example for others and to guide their futures.

An individual who is a legacy may have a better chance of admission to a particular college because their parents or relatives attended. Inheritance, heritage, leaving a legacy means giving something that will be valued and treasured by those who survived after your death. Your legacy is the sum of the personal values, accomplishments, and actions that resonate with the people around you. It's how you made a difference in the world, whether that's building a fortune 500 company or always putting a smile on peoples faces.

Your life story, lessons you've learned, your values and beliefs is called a life legacy. A Life legacy has nothing to do with passing on belongings or money, it's more like leaving a mark with the lessons you've learned in your lifetime for future generations to come. This is the type of man you want to become. Someone who's making a difference, opening doors for others to come through. Let's be real, with the one life you have you can accomplish so much, make mistakes, learn and get right back on track, becoming anything you set your heart out to be. Become the man you know you can for your family sake. Don't dream about it, be a dream chaser. Control your destiny to better the outcome. Take risks, go hard, and stay focused until all goals are met to lock in that Capital.

TRAVIS

Bumped into one of my co-workers named Travis, a really cool guy and I simply asked him what his take on a Perfect

Man is. He quickly said men have to learn how not to be stubborn and listen to their woman sometimes. Consider their ideas and feelings, in some cases men could play the dominant role and not care what women have to say when it comes to controlling the relationship. What he does is surround himself with Knowledgeable people to get their insight on life. What they've been through and how they handle and treat others. That's how he learns how to treat his woman through reasoning to know he's not always right and her wrong.

It doesn't hurt to talk to wise people, you don't have to have all the answers. You ever listen to other people's life stories and think wow mine is not that bad. Sometimes others could face hard times like you but handle things in a different way. Teaching you coping skills you never knew you had, getting you through tough times just by opening your mouth and saying I have a problem I can't solve alone is a start to getting closure when facing difficult situations. I received this lesson just by having a quick conversation by the salad station with my brother Travis. Thanks big T you're a gentleman and a scholar, I salute you.

KIARA

Kiara, a young Server/ Togo Specialist/ Host, always on her ten toes moving running around our three floor restaurant like a bolt of lightning. Kiara, Big not the little one as she states when she grabs the mic to call for silverware and plates. I approached her and asked, young lady, what's your idea of a Perfect Man? Already on the go she quickly darted out a name, Michael B. Jordan as she looked to the heavens like he was coming down to caress her. That's my version of a perfect man, I laughed because her thoughts were obviously fiscal. That's what I sensed from her gesture. Micheal

B. Jordan is a young Talented American actor and producer that played in several highly acclaimed movies such as Creed, Black Panther, Fantastic 4, which all had sequels so he has a "bag", large sum of money. That's what all women seek, a handsome young wealthy man that can change their lives for the better. I think he's taken but if i ever meet him i will be sure to tell him my friend Kiara is looking for him and she is standing on business bout yeah buddy boy, GANG!

TAMARA

Tamara, one of the newest OG servers whose moms is also on the management team. Very bright, light skinned young woman with a big puffy, curly afro that is too cute. She's also tall enough to make it in the WNBA. In college doing well for herself, she only comes and works when she's on a school break. We talk all the time and I always encourage her to keep her grades up and ask her how she's doing when she passes me by in the Ally. She always smiles at me even when she's tired. As and Bs my lady? Yes, Boo As and Bs nothing less she replays. Going right back after summer break trying to make some spending money so i can eat. I totally understood as I asked her my Perfect Man question. She looked at me and said, You!

You're a Perfect Man to me Boo, I was taken back not expecting that answer and she said yes, the way you treat people. You're a great person and your presence when you walk in this building is always love. Everyone loves when you're around, so you're a Perfect Man in my Book. Of course i Thanked her for her kind words and proceeded to tell her why I asked her her thoughts. I'm writing a book to teach all these young men how to move in life. She hit me with a big smile and said, wow that's so needed, best of luck i can't wait to read it. Do I have permission to put your statement in my book? Of course, you don't even have to ask. Love you T-money when you get this blueprint give it to your Boo and tell him if you aint rockin like this i don't want to waste another minute of my time. I'm so serious you deserve a Perfect Man to match your fly, on, God!

The type of man that I am is different from what a lot of people tell me. I'm a real gentleman to the ladies because like I said some beautiful women raised me. I always say I move like Jesus Christ, how caring and kind I am, I really have no hate in my blood unless I feel you're trying to intimidate, or bully me then you'll see my darker side, I'm totally with the shits too. A big giver, let me explain, some people are givers and some are takers. Givers can't get mad at takers because that's what they do. A taker is never scared to ask for what they want from a giver. It's up to the giver to say no which is hard because he or she is a giver. No matter how tired I am, I'll still try to help, even if I don't really got it I'll still give hoping God sees my devotion and blesses me when I'm called home. Mostly for the people I care about even if the love is not reciprocated 100% I still go hard for mine. My little bro John Castro hates that about me. Yo, they are not gonna do that shit for you ma. Let it be, that's just me, I can't change, I don't need consolidation, God got me, please believe me when I tell you. I walk with God on my side, I don't fear and I don't live with regrets. I learn my lessons and move on. If you truly know me, you know that.

MARTIN LAWRENCE

I have some men that I feel are perfect and I look up to and admire and that is, Martin Lawrence and Will Smith.

Martin is an American actor and comedian. He came to fame during the 1990's, establishing a Hollywood career as a leading actor. Born April 16, 1965 in Germany where his father was Stationed. Mother moved him to D.C after divorcing his father where he was raised in the King Square Projects. His mother and brother kept him out of jail because he got into a lot of street fights that landed him into boxing during his teen years. Lawrence excelled at it and became a Mid-Atlantic Golden Gloves boxing contender.

He also was doing Odd jobs like his mother and ended up doing stand-up comedy in the D.C area. A Comedian named Ritch Snyder caught his act and guided him and his talents to, New York City comedy club called The Improv. From there he went on Star Search and lost in the final round. However executives at Columbia Pictures Television saw him and gave him his first big break on What's Happening Now. Do the right thing, House Party 1 and 2, Talkin Dirty After Dark, and then Eddie Murphy Vehicle Boomerang. After that he really took off, salary steadily increasing to over 10 million a show. That man worked so hard that he slipped into a three day coma after collapsing from heat exhaustion while jogging in 100 degree weather, exercising for his role in Big Mommas House. He has Blockbuster Awards, NAACP Awards, Kids Choice awards, MTV Movie Awards, BET Comedy Icon Award, Hollywood Walk Of Fame.

I mean you gotta give respect where respect is due. Ever since I became a father and became a homebody all me and my family watched was Martin the TV show.

The reason why I'm picking Mr Lawrance out of the many talents is because of the Happiness and Punctuality he made me feel with his timeless comedy. He made my day better and I appreciate him for that. He's a gift that kept on giving with all his accolades. Any character, any show, any movie, was the Bomb if he had anything to do with it. Changed my life, a Perfect Man who made everyone around him better, I'm sure you can agree!

WILL SMITH

Will Smith- An American actor, rapper, comedian,songwriter, and film producer. Born September 25, 1968 in Philadelphia. Newsweek called him "the most powerful actor in Hollywood". Smith began his acting career starring as a fictionalized version of himself on the NBC sitcom The Fresh Prince of Bel-Air, which was nominated for the Golden Globe Award for Best Actor. He first gained recognition as part of a Hip-Hop duo with DJ Jazzy Jeff with whom he released five studio albums which contained five Billboard Hot 100 top 20 singles. Parents Just Don't Understand, A Nightmare on my Street, Summertime, Ring my Bell, and Boom Shake the Room in which he won four Grammys.

Smith's parents were also Divorced and his father was in the Air Force. He began rapping at an early age of 12 when his grandmother found a notebook of lyrics, which he described as all his little curse words, she wrote a note on a page in the book: "Dear Willard, truly intelligent people do not have to use words like this to express themselves. Please show the world that you're as smart as we think you are". Smith said that this influenced his decision not to use profanity in his music.

Smith went through a lot, he underpaid his income taxes in 1989, and the internal revenue Service eventually assessed a 2.8 million tax debt against him taking many of his possessions he got from the music and garnished his wages. He was struggling financially in 1990 when NBC television network signed him to a contract and built the Fresh Prince sitcom. Then he set for himself the goal of becoming "The Biggest movie star in the world". He been putting hands on people too, he got arrested for assault on his record promoter the charges were later dismissed. I take it Willy wasn't the man to play with bout his money or family.

First film was Six Degrees of Separation, then Bad Boys, Independence Day, Men in Black, Wild Wild West in which he turned down the Matrix, Muhammed Ali, while doing Albums in between, the list of accolades go on and on. The reason why I boast about Martin and Will is because they are 2 black men that started from nothing and became Icons in their own right. Bad boys 4 grossed $104 million dollars in the first day, 456 in America and $48 international. They are still goin, Martian got a Stand up tour hitting Barclay and Atlantic City soon and Will is about to come out with I am Legend 2 and Handcock 2. 1 don't know about yall but if they talk, i'm listening. Mo' money, Mo' money, Mo' money!

THE KING

If we are talking about the Perfect Man then i have to talk about this King, LeBron James. Four Championships, 19 all-Star game nominations and an imminent coronation as the NBAs all-time leading scorer. That's just basketball but its James' ambitious pursuits off-the-court that may ultimately distinguish his legacy from other athletes.

LeBron James Started a scholarship and counseling Family Foundation that put almost 200 people through college thus far. He has helped and served more than 1,500 students and their entire families by providing them with the fundamental resources, wraparound support and family programming they need for success in schools and beyond.(LJFF) LeBron James Family Foundation.

James also Co-founded a successful media and entertainment company, bought stakes in storied professional baseball and soccer franchises and, with a big assist from product endorsements, his net worth is estimated to have grown above $1 billion. The off-court achievements that James is most proud of, he says, is working to uplift lives. Many athletes have excelled in one or more of these areas. But few have done all of them as well as James, who is closing in on passing Kareem Abdul-Jabbar for the NBAs career scoring record. "His goal, I believe, is to have 10% of his wealth go to causes and support communities, which is an amazing goal," He's going above and beyond others, just in that aspiration.

Another amazing feat that i'm glad i lived to witness that i've never seen in my life is the signing of his oldest son Bronny James to the Lakers for a guaranteed $7.9 million 4 year deal in which LeBron just signed for another 2 years so him and his son could play on the same team, unbelievable. Who's going to be a better mentor than his own father who has now played 21 total seasons in the NBA to date. The chance to throw his son an alley-oop in an official game like they do at home is crazy.

BOUNDARIES

Boundaries- Show where one thing ends and another begins. Boundaries in a relationship are kind of like this, they help each person figure out where one person ends and another begins. In short, boundaries help you define what you are comfortable with and how you would like to be treated by others.

Personal Healthy Boundaries are being able to say "no" and accept when someone else says "no". Being able to clearly communicate both wants and needs. Honoring and respecting their own needs and the needs of others. Respecting others values, beliefs, and opinions, even if they are different from one's own. When you set boundaries in a relationship, be calm, firm, and clear and reasonable on consequences for crossing a boundary. If someone has a habit of talking over you, for example, you could say, "I feel disrespected when you talk over me. If you do that again, I'll have to end this conversation."

A person with no boundaries will feel that others don't respect him, He feels used, by giving a lot and not receiving back, He has no privacy, He can overshare everything about his life, and He will always try to seek approval from others. Some key examples of boundaries in a relationship are expecting others to communicate during disagreements with maturity. Letting go of codependency and having your own identity. Asking for personal space and quiet when you're working. Voicing your concerns rather than holding onto resentment.

Boundaries can include anything from telling someone you don't have time to talk right now to letting someone know you aren't going to lend them money. At first boundaries feel uncomfortable. You might worry that you've hurt someone's feelings or that they'll be upset with you. If someone is manipulating you, be assertive and set personal boundaries, so you know what you will tolerate. If you need to confront manipulators, identify the negative behaviors that you've observed, and be specific about how their actions harm the relationship.

GOALS

Goals- The Object of a person's ambition or effort, to aim for desired results. The desired states that people seek to obtain, maintain, or avoid in their work, relationship, finances, health, and personal development. It involved identifying desired outcomes and developing a plan for achieving them, which can provide long-term direction and short-term motivation.

Finding a career that you love or a life partner, becoming an expert or leader in your field. How about going for a walk every day, becoming a better listener, buying your first home. Save x amount of dollars for retirement, give back to your community in ways that matter to you. These are all personal goals that a person could take on to better their lives.

When I was younger one of my most important goals was to work hard to be a better father than my own. Then I had to get a High School Diploma for my aunt on to a life for my kids. Goals don't stop, you can make a new one everyday but the key is to see them through to the end. It'll fill you with so much gratitude that you accomplished what you set out to do in a timely manner. Goals big or small can change your life for the better. Pushing yourself, working your mind like an exercise thinking of goals to reach brings improvement. Getting more money is a Goal, starting your own business becoming a Boss is a goal. Taking a very needed vacation to a hot beautiful island, Clearing up your debt, losing weight are all goals that you can set for yourself to reach.

Motivational goals can inspire you and help you find value in achieving them. If you're not motivated, you might not put in the effort to make your goals happen. Focusing on goals can help you know where you're headed and give you a map to start on. Tracking your progress can also help you stay focused and meet deadlines. Goals are necessary to win in a big way, your way, your rules, your pace.

MOTIVATION

Motivation, The reason one has for acting or behaving in a particular way. The general desire or willingness of someone to do something. My kids and family are my motivation, I work myself to the bone so they can eat and enjoy what life has to offer. Motivation is the desire to act in service of a goal. Its the crucial element in attaining our objectives. Motivation is one of the driving forces behind human behavior. It fuels competition and sparks social connection. Its absence can lead to mental illnesses such as depression.

Motivation refers to a process of inducing and stimulating an individual to act in a certain manner. In the context of an organization, motivation implies encouraging and urging the employees to perform to the best of their capabilities so as to achieve the desired goals of the organization. Posting a picture up on the wall of an athlete you love then practicing their skill to become great or greater than them is motivation. The Perfect Man needs to be motivated to reach all his goals to be successful. It is the engine that controls the spirit and gives you the willpower to give it your best.

A wise Bossman can motivate a whole team by giving them rewards for goals reached like full paid vacations or time and a half on their salary. Free dinners or movie passes, pictures of the leading team member of the month, days off, free clothing or work attire, Raises. An organization can crumble without a little motivation. It's the key to self devotion and success.

DETERMINATION

Determination, the commitment to achieve your goals, regardless of the challenges you might experience. It often includes being decisive and demonstrating resoluteness. People who express determination continue to work to achieve their goals, regardless of other factors. The ability to continue trying to do something although it is very difficult. Determination is like a great boxing match in which both opponents don't want to lose but it can only be one winner. The one with the most determination will dig deep and find a way to get the knockout. It's a must have ability for the Perfect man to learn. I hope I'm opening the eyes of my young readers and giving you what you need to push through to the top. I am determined to get these lessons into every lost young Brain in the world. It's normal to be frustrated or disappointed at times, but if you're determined, you do your best to achieve success.

FOCUS

Focus- The full meaning of focus, a center of activity, attraction, or attention. When a person is focused on something, they're paying attention to it. When a camera lens or your eyes are focused, they've made the

adjustments needed to see clearly. Another word for focus is concentration. You have to Focus all your concentration on your goals. Focused people tend to be highly motivated, disciplined and persistent in pursuing their goals. Prioritizing their time and energy towards activities that align with their goals and values. Focus is the link to all sorts of decision making, problem-solving, reasoning, learning, memory, and perception needs. If you're unable to focus well, it will negatively impact your ability to think. Knowing how to focus and concentrate all your efforts on something can be life-changing, Know that!

Music could make you focus on a task, Cooking, cleaning, working out, or dancing. Help you get into the groove for sex, or relax your brain to take your focus off your problems and think about something else like the first time you heard a song, where you were, who you were with and how you felt at that moment good or bad times, life or death music is a vessel for focusing and that's a fact. I mean try it, put on some tunes and see how far it will take you.

How to improve your focus, cut out disruption to create a distraction free zone. Do one thing at a time, practice mindfulness to strengthen your focus muscle. Prioritize good sleep to keep your focus sharp. Stay in the now, and don't worry about the next task. That's one thing I just learned, sleep is so important you are supposed to get 8 hours of sleep at least. I ain't sleep in 25 years burning myself out over focused on working to take care of my family. Some say if you sleep all day you're not getting to the bag, but if you burn yourself out, you may see an early grave. I have to learn how to focus on a better me, better organize my time and energy. You know, get focused!

DRIVE

Drive- If you say that someone has drive, you mean they have energy and determination. A driven individual is someone who is highly motivated and determined to achieve their goals. They are often characterized by their strong work ethic, their willingness to put in the extra effort, and their ability to stay focused on their goals even when things get tough. Drive, which can also be viewed as action and commitment, is what is going to get you to that end goal. It will keep you going even when your motivation comes to a halt. Drive, essentially, is what will keep moving you forward when there's a dip in motivation.

Strong determination to do or achieve something, intelligence isn't enough you've got to have that drive to succeed. All jokes to the left, have you ever started something and didnt finish, and you had to get your drive back to complete that task. Once you did it, your life changed, you learned that skill and moved on to the next level, they call that leveling up. Drive is that power force inside you that doesn't allow you to quit or cheat yourself out of that lesson. That thing that makes you say F that I'm doing this with no regrets and no turning back. I gotta see this thing till the end, if i don't i'll have to live with that what if for the rest of my life.

The other form of drive is operating a vehicle, something that can move you from one spot to another in less time it takes you to walk or run. To drive legally you must go to the DMV, The Department of Motor Vehicles to get you a driver's license. Driving fosters a sense of responsibility and independence from having to rely on busy parents or family members. Learning to maintain a vehicle and manage vehicle expenses is good practice for the responsibilities of adulthood. The main reason I love to drive is because it increases my hustle to another level. I can make faster moves to get to the money. I can hit multiple businesses in a day. Catch up to people that are busy and don't have time to waste waiting for me to get to them by mass transit. Make my rounds and be back at home in time for dinner, so to speak.

When I was young I couldn't wait to drive. I used to steal,I mean borrow my aunt's red Geo Prizm and ride around my town. One time I hopped out at the park and locked her keys in the car hanging out the ignition. The police were right across the street and had to help me back into the car with a slim jim before they could ask for my license.I was gone. I didn't have one to show anyway. I was only 13, made it back home, parked the car and put her keys back before she woke up. To my point I had driven around half the Bronx in an hour. The Perfect Man has to have a valid driver's license in his wallet to make moves. Time is money, and my family love taking trips and going places.

PHILL

I stopped a young man named Phill at work today and asked him my infamous question. Phill, i'm in the midst of writing a book called the Perfect Man. What is a Perfect Man to you, what are your thoughts? To my delight his answer was sweeter than pumpkin pie covered with whip cream and cinnamon. Phill looked me dead in my eyes and said, the perfect man has to be a man that is slow to anger, mindful of other people's space. He has to be a man of respect and wisdom. No one could make him do anything they wanted him to do. He's in full control of any situation, totally has a mind of his own and can stand on his own 2 feet. Intelligent and strong, people need him for guidance. He has a heart made of pure gold and willing to help anyone that asks for it. Everyone rocks with him because they know he speaks from the heart.

Ok, he said the first 3 lines because we were working but I knew where he was going so I used my writing skills to fill in the blanks with Phill's permission of course. I got you and Thank you my young brother. I don't know who raised

Phill, but I will hang with him one day and find out his story. Whoever did it, They did an awesome job. He has the skills to be a Perfect Man so I was glad I stopped him and gave him some lines in the book. Very cool and respectful, gets along with everyone and I wish him well on his journey of life, He's definitely going places.

The Perfect Man according to the Bible, "without flaw,' that is no imperfections. Under the covenant, Abraham had met some conditions. He had to live a life of obedience. He had to submit to God. God raised the standard so high for him, that one would almost think he had to be without sin.

YE FASHAN

Ye Fashan or Yeh Fa-shan also known as Perfect Man Ye, was a Taoist wonder-worker reportedly from the Tang Dynasty. According to hagiographic legend, he ascended to Heaven as an immortal "in broad daylight." July, 720. I wasn't there so i don't know, i'm just stating the facts that were written, DON'T shoot the messenger!

JILLIAN & JADEN

Jillian and Jaden are a young couple that met at the job, Olive Garden Times square. Both were Hosts that had the opportunity to become servers to better their future. At some point love filled the air for them and they are now looking forward to a new edition to all our lives. See, when a couple has a child, that baby becomes an OG baby for life. We all kinda give love and support as a unit. That's one thing that is true with the, when you're here your family quote. So Congratulations to them, they are happily expecting a beautiful baby girl. It's the couple's very first child.and every one so anxious to see her especially Jillian. She is tired and ready to pop, Jaden is taking it in stride, one day at a time doing any and everything to make his soon to be baby momma comfortable and happy which is a job in itself.

We are a family, they are like my children so me being a cook here I feed them any chance I get. Especially Jillian because she's eating for two and working so I gotta make sure her energy is good. Today she was getting some soup so I figured she had the munchies. I had an extra artichoke dip that I persuaded her to grab. When she came to say hi and thank me for the gesture i took an opportunity to rub her belly and give the baby some love. That's when I told her about what I was doing my book for and I slid the question in like a pitcher on a mound. Jillian, what is a Perfect Man to you? She smiled and thought, then she said i have a lot to say so i gave her a pencil and paper to let her express her thoughts in her own time.

An Hour went by and I tracked her down and asked her what she came up with. With a glow in her eyes she told me straight up that her answer was related to Jaden and their relationship, on how much he loved her so crazy that he is a Perfect Man to her. That made me very proud of him and so excited for them both. Just to know their daughter is coming into a loving couple brought me so much joy. I had a damn proud father moment myself, but she wasn't done so i left her to continue her thoughts. This in her true words is what she came up with,

A man that knows how to let it be known that he's in a relationship with you, with his loyalty only to his partner.

A man who knows that not everything in life comes easy, he knows that hard work and dedication is the way.

A lot of Patience!

A man who lives to serve not only himself but everyone around him, not afraid to show emotions and be vulnerable.

A man who provides and is reliable because he wants to be and not because hes obligated.

A man who knows a relationship is based on so much more than physical, not just all about sex.

A man who has faith in a higher power such as God.

A man who is not overly materialistic.

A man who does not overly indulge in drugs or alcohol.

A man that does not lust in another woman in any kind of way.

A man who can recognize when another woman is crossing boundaries and shut it down.

Go head Jillian that's how you feel, I can dig it. I'm going to nickname the baby Lovely because that's what I think you guys' relationship is. Stay pure and kind to each other, Uncle Boo will be around.

MR. DAVID

My BossMan David had this to say, A Perfect Man should be a Leader, responsible and trustworthy. When he said that I laughed because he was so militant I kinda knew what his answer would be. He once was an officer I think he said a Chief. Mr David is always straight up and helpful, a great man to work with. Officers live by a perfect guideline to uphold the law you have to be in the streets but not of it. He definitely works by code and is dedicated to whatever it is he's interested in. I wouldn't say he's a tightwad, he can look the other way. Everything is not that serious, but don't disrespect him, I don't think you want to see that darkside in him. I'm sure he busted a few guns in his day. He's also raising a son, so I hope when I get this book selling it gets into his son's hand. He's definitely the kind of young man I'm trying to reach.

PATIENCE

Patience - The ability to wait, or to continue doing something despite difficulties, or to suffer without complaining or becoming annoyed. You have to have a lot of patience when you are dealing with kids or childish adults. Patience is when you exercise self-control rather than lashing out and complaining. You're being patient when you take deep breaths and seek inner peace after things don't go the way you hoped. Practicing patience is all about how you act.

Having patience means you can remain calm, even when you've been waiting forever or dealing with something painstakingly slow or trying to teach someone how to do something and they just don't get it. It involves acceptance and tolerance, and is usually easier to have when there's something in it for you at the end.

As a child going through a lot of trauma, never getting anything easy, I developed a tremendous amount of patience. Spending a lot of time alone traveling through New York, working, grinding, learning people, who to trust, who not to. My struggle made me patient, building myself into the man I am today, surviving, raising a family. All of these things created my patience. Stress at work, stress at home, burning my candle on both ends would have made me go insane a long time ago. My patience and trust in God with a lot of woosahing, kept me out of jail. That's why this new generation needs to get a fresh start on life, do the right things to stay focused by surrounding yourself with only positive people that can help you build so you can have way less stress and much more success, Good luck!

What is forgiveness? Forgiveness means different things to different people. But in general, it involves an intentional decision to let go of resentment and anger. The act that hurt or offended you might always be with you but forgiveness will set your heart at ease and let your mind be free. My Dad wasn't a Dad so I in return wasn't a son, he passed before we could talk and forgive each other. I wish we did, I'm sorry we didn't and that's something I have to deal with for the rest of my life. I don't really know him. I don't fully know myself and all the things I'm capable of through him and that's sad. For my reader, do yourself a favor if you have it in your heart to forgive someone that wronged you, do it and move on. Life is too short to cry over spilled milk. You can forgive but never forget, just move accordingly and live. Karmas a Bitch, so just trust everything will work out in your favor. On God!

HAILE SELASSIE MUHAMMED

Muhammed (born c. 570, Mecca, Arabia {now in Saudi Arabia}- died June 8, 632, Medina) was the founder of Islam and the proclaimer of the Qur'an. Because Muhammed was the chosen recipient and messenger of the word of God through the divine revelations, Muslims from all walks of life strive to follow his word. As he was the most influential Perfect Man in the world.

The Prophet Muhammad- Historically, it was Muhammed (alaihissalam) peace be upon him. He was recognised even by his enemies as a most sincere, trustworthy, morally perfect person. He has had so much empathy for every creature, even when he was beaten, thrown stones on his head by the people of a city, he prayed for them, he forgave them. He never lied in his life, even when joking. He never had food in his home more than for one day, because he was giving almost everything in charity. He expressed in a few words so much, his good character, some minutes or hours spent with him were enough for people to choose to accept the religion of islam he was explaining. Every companion thought himself as the closest person to Muhammed (messenger of Allah).Because they received so much love, help, consideration from him. He was a religious leader, teacher, wonderful loving husband and father, king of justice, an example for every generation who lived after him, the most wonderful, perfect human being. We should also mention that he was very good looking physically. Billions followed him, loved him. Generations before him were waiting for his arrival, announced in old and new Testaments. Generations who saw him with their eyes were the luckiest ones. He is still the leader, the exemplary person for billions right now. No doubt, he was the most perfect, the most influential, most loved and wonderful human being of all times.

The first word revealed to our Prophet Muhammed from Allah was "Iqra" which means to read! To seek knowledge! Educate yourself! Be Educated.

There is no such thing as a perfect man-all men, and women, are flawed. But, if you want to become a good man, my suggestion to you is this…

1. Become dangerous.

2. Learn self-control.

When it comes to being a good man you need to be able to do a few things. Protect, Provide, and Lead.

Protect yourself and those you love.

Provide for a family.

Lead others by example.

To accomplish these things you must become dangerous…

Dangerous of both mind and body.

You must train yourself to be quick thinking.

You must train yourself to be strategic.

You must train yourself to adapt.

You must train yourself to fight.

If you want to be able to protect loved ones and provide for them, you need to become strong both physically and mentally.

Learn to lift weights.

Learn how to punch and take someone down to the ground.

Learn to shoot a gun.

Learn how to negotiate.

Learn how to think two steps ahead.

Learn how to be calm in a chaotic environment.

But if you choose to become a good man, there is another very important part. The line between a good man and a very bad man lies in one key characteristic…

Self-control.

A good man can control the power of his thoughts, actions, and words.

A bad man gives in to his emotions and his desires.

A good man knows how to delay gratification.

A bad man wants everything now.

A good man does things for the gain of others.

A bad man does things for his own gain.

A good man uses his power to influence others positively

A bad man uses his power to influence others negatively.

Being harmless doesn't help anyone.

You can't protect yourself and not others.

Being dangerous allows you to protect, provide, and lead.

But being dangerous must be balanced with self-control.

If not you will cross the line and become the exact thing you were trying to avoid.

Self-control is the ability to control oneself, in particular one's emotions and desires or the expression of them in one's behavior, especially in difficult situations.

No one can control you, no one can make you sell drugs, fight, steal, or in the worst case scenario, kill when you practice self-control. Be your own man, control your own destiny. If anyone or anything disrupts that motion, change your circumstances by noticing the problem and fixing it. Change your friends, make your circle safe.

TAXES

Taxes- A compulsory contribution to state revenue, levied by the government on workers income and business profits, or added to the cost of some goods, services, and transactions.

A tax is a mandatory payment or charge collected by local, state, and national governments from individuals or businesses to cover the costs of general government services, goods, and activities.

Taxes provide revenue for federal, local. and state government to fund essential services, defense, highways, police, a justice system that benefit all citizens, who could not provide such services very effectively for themselves.

There are several very common types of taxes:

Income tax- A percentage of generated income that is relinquished to the state or federal government.

Payroll tax- A percentage withheld from an employee's pay by the employer, who pays it to the government on the employee's behalf to fund Medicare and Social Security programs.

Paying taxes is an indicator that you are earning income, generally speaking which is a positive thing. A lot of taxes usually equals a lot of money. Since paying taxes is the law, its something that legally must be done. Even if you have your own business you have to pay your taxes.

The most common forms of business are the sole proprietorship, partnership, corporation, and S corporation. A limited liability company (LLC) is a business structure allowed by state statute. Legal and tax considerations enter into selecting a business structure.

The reason why taxes are most important to stay on top of for me is the fact that if handled wrongly you can face some severe consequences. The government can shut your businesses down, garnish your income, or at worst give you time in jail. Just me trying to hit all angles of information for a man to know when going into business for themselves. Knowledge is really power so stay on top of your game. Running a business is not an easy task, I'm a great cook. Everyone is always telling me to open a restaurant or get a food truck, but they don't want to invest and provide the thousands of dollars it takes just to get off the ground. All the licenses, the grants I may need to apply for, the team I need to require for the support I need to be successful. It takes a lot, not saying it can't happen, anything is possible but be real when you approach me. Hey i got 10 grand how much you got? Let's get this business going. I got your back, maybe then i'll take a listen and be interested in what you have to say.

FINANCIAL AID

Financial aid- funds from the government, private organizations and / or from an educational institution to help students pay for their education. There are various types of financial aid including grants, work-study, loans and scholarships. The type of aid you receive after filling out the FAFSA determines if you need to pay it back. Grants, scholarships, and work-study money doesn't need to be repaid but has finite funding limits. You will need to repay subsidized, unsubsidized, and Direct Plus Loans.

Your financial aid office will apply your aid to the amount you owe your school and send you the balance to spend on other college costs. One of the requirements to maintain financial aid eligibility is that you must make satisfactory academic progress, And don't forget to complete a FAFSA form each year!

Money that is given to someone in order to help them. Aid is money, equipment, or services that are provided for people, countries, or organizations who need them but cannot provide them for themselves. You can choose to get paid by check or direct deposit, or have the money credited to your school account to pay for your education-related charges (such as tuition, fees, and room and board).

Types of Financial Aid

Federal Vs Private Loans

Grants

Subsidized and Unsubsidized

Federal Student Loans

Scholarships

Federal financial and regulation states that if you withdraw from all of your classes or cease enrollment prior to the 60 percent point of instruction in any term, you will be required to repay all unearned financial aid funds received. A calculation will be performed to determine the repayment amount.The Department of Education does not have an official income cutoff to qualify for federal financial aid so if you feel your parents income is too high, it's still worth applying for, to apply is free so go for it. Number one goal in life which is proven to be true is your education.

PASSPORT

Passport- A formal document issued by an authorized official of a country to one of the citizens that is usually necessary for exit from and reentry into the country, that allows the citizen to travel in a foreign country in accordance with visa requirements, and that requests protection for citizens while abroad.

A U.S. passport is your ticket to international travel. The U.S. passport is a request to foreign governments to permit you to travel or temporarily reside in their territories and have access to lawful local aid and protection. The passport allows you access to U.S. consular services and assistance while abroad.

It takes 6 to 8 weeks routine

Expedited 2 to 3 weeks and an extra $60 cash

Urgent Travel u must find a nearby Passport office and pay in person.

People use passports for Business travel, most importantly vacations. All the beautiful islands you see on Instagram and Facebook come from people with their passports. I didn't play. I got a passport and a passport card. When i go away I keep my card on me, and my passport in the hotel I chose to stay at. I'm getting home, please believe it. These islands are lovely but that's not my home, anything pops off I don't understand and yea boy on the next flight out. Key factor, try to check the weather before you make flight arrangements. Make sure you're not flying into a tornado or bad storm when you land, you will be stuck.

If you're a businessman and you're doing business abroad because that's how you roll. Make sure your accounts are active for your big money transfers. You don't want any issues when you are spending or receiving that Shmoney!

TIME

Time, the measured or measurable period during which an action, process, or condition exists or continues. Physicists define the progression of events from the past to the present into the future. Basically, if a system is unchanging, it is timeless. Time can be considered to be the fourth dimension of reality, used to describe events in three-dimensional space.

Time is an important concept because it is a fundamental aspect of our existence and the world around us. Time allows us to measure the duration of events, the sequence of actions, and the rate of change. It is also a valuable resource that cannot be replaced or replenished, making it a limited and precious commodity.

The purpose of time is to provide a way of measuring and ordering events and processes. Time enables us to track changes, to compare durations, and to predict future occurrences. It allows us to coordinate our activities with others, to plan for the future, and to reflect on the past.

I don't play with my time. Time is of the essence, only time will tell, don't lose track of time, I ain't got time for this, what, a time we had, I need a little more time, what time are we leaving tomorrow, things get better with time, what time is it?

Time is everything, it's all we have to keep us on track. It moves so fast it can make you feel like you're running out of it. So much to do and so little time. Time is so precious that we have to try and enjoy every minute of it. Spend time with your loved ones, do the things that you want to do because life is short. Travel, see the world, ashes to ashes and dust to dust we'll all be has -beens so make the best of your time and live the best you can. Time is the greatest teacher of them all. Be aware of that and move like there's no tomorrow. It's hard for me to do that but if you know me, you know I try.

PREPARATION

Preparation is the act of preparing- getting ready, planning, training or studying with a goal in mind. If you know pre means before, then you have a clue to the meaning of preparation. Dressing up before a date, learning your lines for a play, and attending medical school are forms of preparation. To make yourself ready to deal with a difficult situation. Getting something ready for use or for a particular purpose or making arrangements for something.

Preparation is something that must be done to secure your future. If you stay ready, you don't have to get ready. Getting your clothes out for school in the morning. Inspecting your car before a road trip, very important for safe travels. Cultivate a "growth mindset." Hone your time management skills. Start thinking in terms of your career. Budget your money. Save for the future. Establish good credit. Improve your communication skills. Cook your own meals occasionally.

If you plan ahead and make sure you have everything you need the night before, your day will go more smoothly, and that's a fact.

ENDURANCE

Endurance, the ability to persist or persevere through challenges, difficulties, or hardships over the course of one's lifetime. It implies a sense of resilience and tenacity, as well as a willingness to endure discomfort or pain in order to achieve a goal or overcome an obstacle. The ability to keep doing something difficult, unpleasant, or painful for a long time.

You build endurance by running as regularly as you can. Be consistent with your schedule, running at least three to four times a week. The exact number of runs depends on your running experience and fitness levels. Beginner runners should start small with only one or two runs per week, allowing for your body to adapt.

Playing sports regularly would also help, constant movement helps your heart give you better blood flow. I'm writing this book and learning as I go myself. Preparation and Endurance are more skills for the Perfect Man to achieve greatness. Practice makes perfect so make everyday a learning process, give everything you learn time and you will see a change immediately.

STEVE JOBS

Poignant last words of Steve Jobs, billionaire dead at 56:

"I have reached the pinnacle of success in business." In other people's eyes my life is a success. However, aside from work, I've had little joy. At the end of the day, wealth is just a fact I've gotten used to. Right now, lying on my hospital bed, reminiscing all my life. I realize that all the recognition and wealth I took so much pride in, has faded and become meaningless in the face of imminent death.

You can hire someone to drive your car or make money for you, but you can't hire someone to stand sick and die for you. Material things lost can be found again. But there is one thing that can't be found when its lost: Life. Whatever stage of life we are currently at, in time we will face the day the curtain closes. Love your family, spouse, children and friends... Treat them right.

Cherish them.

As we get older, and wiser, we slowly realize that wearing a $300 or $30 watch both give the same time.

Whether we have a $300 or $30 wallet or purse, the amount inside is the same.

Whether we drive a $150,000 car or a $30,000 car, the road and the distance are the same, and we reach the same destination.

Whether we drink a $1000 or $10 bottle of wine, the hangover is the same.

Whether the house in which we live is 100 or 1000 square meters, loneliness is the same.

You will realize that your true inner happiness does not come from material things of this world.

Whether you travel first class or economy class, if the plane crashes, you go down with it...

Therefore, I hope you realize, when you have friends, brothers and sisters, with whom you discuss, laugh, talk, sing, talk about north-south-east or heaven and earth,...This is the real happiness!

An indisputable fact of life:

Don't raise your children to be rich. Educate them to be happy. When they grow up, they will know the value of things and not the price."

If im keeping it real, then I had to put Mr. Jobs last words in my book. It was so real that I had to let it live on. He touched me, his words let me know that you can have all the money in the world but if you're not in tune with your loved one's it's worth nothing in the end. Money doesn't make you happy and wealth is just that, wealth. Thank you Mr. Jobs you're still a Perfect Man in my book, SIP!

As my book comes to a close, I had a ton of fun researching and putting all this Brain information together for this new generation to study and change the way they see life. Change the game, that's the bottom line. Have some respect for women and yourself. Treat people with the utmost respect, you don't know what no one is going through behind closed doors. They may be at the end of their rope and they're ready to take you and everyone else out around them. Don't be a victim, stay active, keep that engine running and your mind focused on the end goal. A well rounded successful young man that takes care of his loved ones physically and financially with happiness and joy.

AFTERWORD

I hope I touched every topic known to man that can groom a man into someone special. I see a lot of kids on the train wielding smoking weed, disrespecting their elders not caring if they go to jail or get killed is crazy. Noted, the big momma era is gone, grandmothers are 28 years old and babies are having babies. This was all inspiration to me to take notice and write something of circumstance. Touch the people, make a legacy for me and my kids. Something that can teach and reach the masses, as long as we have books to read and words to say, say them from the heart and stand on what you say.

I love you all and I hope you love this blueprint.

The Perfect Man

ABOUT THE AUTHOR

The older I get, the more I appreciate how I was raised and who raised me. Born in the Bronx and raised in the hood had its challenges. I've had plenty of men in and out my life but all of them were far from perfect. I was raised on T V personalities Like The Cosby show, The Jeffersons, Sanford and son. I learned from a young age to be successful you had to work because no one was going to hand you anything on a platter. No this ain't no, I'm not raised with a silver spoon story at all. I had kids early and only accomplished a High School Diploma, not embarrassed but I should've pushed for more and got a higher education. I jumped straight into work and it was hard. As far back as I can remember I've been chasing the bag when I should have had the bag chasing me. " Smart people can play dumb but dumb people can't play smart," Gervonta Davis. So I wasn't dumb I just thought to do what my father didn't and spoil my kids and be there for them financially and emotionally. I never ran from my problems and my responsibilities. I faced them head on which was overwhelmingly stressful but everyone had their share of problems so who am I to complain.

I live by if you made your bed you gotta lay in it, Ten toes down, lead by example, I know the people that know me understand where i'm going with this. I never worry about people I don't know or go places i'm not wanted. I'm at where I'm at, and I'll be where I'll be. To Know me is to love me and I spread love everywhere I go so people vibe with me and love to have me in their space and life. I was raised with respect and love so that's what I intend to receive or you can definitely miss me because I'll never need you more than you'll need me. Matter of fact if you helped me once i probably helped you 50 times. My friends are my family and I don't play about that. It takes alot to cross me but when I'm done, I'm done. I will act like you're dead and walk past you like I never knew your name. I can kill with kindness or silence and I don't need no one in my life acting funny money.

That's me, Louis Curtis McCray Jr (BOO)

I wrote this book for the young man who wants to build himself and the mothers who don't have fathers to teach their sons how to be a man, because she's definitely not one. I hope The Perfect Man helps in any form or fashion, and I hope I touched some key topics that make a change to the new Generations of young men to come who may be lost and want to do better but were never really spoken to on a man to man basis. May God keep us all safe in his love and we live to love one another again through Knowledge of self and compassion. Endless love, and the more you read you will improve your speech and communication skills so don't be embarrassed to open a book on a bus or train woman like that Gentleman. Speak from the heart and let your sound, mind, and body be free to grow. Protect your Peace, Boo love and I'm out!